Bob Flowerdew's
Complete Book of
Companion Gardening

BOB FLOWERDEW'S
COMPLETE BOOK OF
COMPANION
GARDENING

Photographs by Jacqui Hurst

KYLE CATHIE LIMITED

A note on the naming of plants

To make for a more readable text, plants are referred to by their most commonly used name whenever possible. Common names are written without a capital letter unless they are also personal names or places: violet, Worcesterberry, St John's wort. When there is any danger of misunderstanding or when it is important to know the exact genus or species, I have used the Latin name. To save repetition the generic name may be abbreviated to its initial: *Euphorbia lactea*, *E. lathyrus*. If only the generic name is used, then any comment applies to the whole genus, but where it is followed with a species name it tells us which specific member of a genus we are talking about. Thus *Malus* refers to the entire apple genus, while *Artemisia absinthium* is specifically wormwood.

For the benefit of North American readers, zone numbers are given throughout the text as a guide to the hardiness of perennial plants. The US Department of Agriculture map which illustrates these zones and their average temperature ranges is reproduced on p. 170.

First published in Great Britain in 1993 by
Kyle Cathie Limited
3 Vincent Square London SW1P 2LX

Copyright © 1993 by Bob Flowerdew
Photographs copyright © 1993 by Jacqui Hurst

ISBN 1 85626 054 2

A CIP catalogue record for this book is available from the British Library

Designed by Geoff Hayes
Edited by Caroline Taggart
Index compiled by the author with the help of Christine Topping
American gardening consultant Charles Cresson
Colour reproduction by Daylight Colour Art Pte Ltd, Singapore
Printed and bound in Great Britain by the Bath Press

I would like to dedicate this book to my father, Richard Flowerdew, without whose support so little would have been possible.

Bob Flowerdew
Dickleburgh
Norfolk

An early example of companion planting

I once saw an old man who had a few acres of abandoned land, the soil too poor for ploughing or grazing and unfit for vines. Yet he planted pot-herbs here and there amid the scrub, and around them white lilies, verbena and scanty poppies, by his energy he matched the wealth of kings. As he came home at night he would pile his table high with unbought produce. He was the first to pick roses in spring, and apples in autumn. He was the first to abound in full-grown bees and a powerful swarm, to squeeze the combs and gather the fermenting honey. Limes he had and laurustinus in plenty. As many were the fruits which the vigorous tree clad herself with in early blossoming as were retained full ripe in autumn. He planted out late elm-shoots in rows, and plums already fruiting and planes giving shade to drinkers.

Virgil, *Georgics IV*, 31 BC
(abridged from James Rhoades' translation, London 1881)

CONTENTS

INTRODUCTION: WHAT IS COMPANION GARDENING?

New ideas take a long time to be accepted, especially in gardening. It sometimes seems as if 'the establishment' opposes any innovation until its worth has been proved absolutely beyond doubt. In the same way, old methods which have been 'improved upon' or rendered 'obsolete' by technology are often discarded wholesale, regardless of whether or not they might still be an appropriate solution to a particular problem. But these abandoned techniques can rise again. Organic and biodynamic approaches to gardening were once seen as eccentric and of marginal interest, with no practical application. Now they are recognized as both desirable and efficient, combining real quality with long-term sustainability.

Companion gardening is a similar case. Many of the companion effects described in this book are utilized every day by gardeners everywhere (whether they realize it or not) and some have been practised since classical times – yet otherwise rational, competent authorities scathingly deny that there is any basis to them. But although we cannot always explain why companion effects work, the fact remains that they do, and with care and observation we can learn to use them to our advantage. We must aim to work with nature rather than against her.

The science of companion gardening is in its infancy. We are just beginning to discover how many interesting and potentially useful interactions there are between different plants, between plants and animals, and between plants and their environment. But with the move towards greener lifestyles, this process is bound to accelerate.

In these last years of the twentieth century, we are in grave danger of destroying our life-support system. Ecology teaches us that we can no longer consider plants, the soil, wildlife, pests and diseases in isolation. They are inextricably linked, as we are

linked to them. Life on this planet is part of one great whole, and any loss is a loss to us all.

Being a companion gardener means consciously planning not only which plants you are going cultivate, but also which other plants you are going to grow them with. Biodynamic and most organic gardeners use companion planting as an intrinsic part of their methods, and many other gardeners unwittingly use companion effects much of the time; indeed, some of their best practices are based on them. But they go unrecognized simply because they are so commonplace.

Essentially companion planting is about the interactions of different plants growing in close proximity. The traditional example is chives growing under roses, with the chives helping the roses to resist blackspot and increasing their perfume. Another much quoted example is that onions never do well with beans and vice versa. But some companion effects are even more basic than that. Weed control is entirely concerned with minimizing negative companion effects, especially those arising from competition for light and space. Crop rotation, which is employed in most productive gardens, is a companion effect over time; one crop is chosen to follow another because it will benefit from the conditions the first crop leaves behind. Orchards and pastures are sown with mixtures of beneficial companions, while the invaluable Tagetes marigold features in almost every bedding display.

The effect of direct plant interaction is only one facet of companion gardening: there are myriad other relationships going on all the time, some of them unseen beneath the surface of the garden. Pollination and pollinators, pests and predators, competition for nutrients, the interplay of all the forms of life within the soil – the companion gardener must try to understand as much of this as possible so that plants can be used effectively to improve their environment, microclimate and soil, and to attract and provide shelter and food for other forms of life, which in turn benefit the plants.

The most important thing is to be good companions ourselves, to be perfect hosts. It is essential to give every plant exactly the right type of soil, shelter, aspect and treatment, with extra help while it establishes itself. This requires intimate knowledge of the plant's requirements and a fair understanding of your garden's different microclimates – which spots are hot and dry, which are cool and moist and so on.

With companion planting we consider whether or not a plant will get on well in any given place and especially with its immediate and potential neighbours. We also look to all the other relationships it may have. The weed and shade competition mentioned above is one. Replant disease – poor growth common in a plant put in or near where one of the same genus has recently been – is another. So the soil condition, microlife and fertility left by previous crops all affect the way following plants respond and these effects may persist for several years.

Another everyday interaction between plants is pollination. This is absolutely critical for almost all fruits, nuts and berries and for many vegetable crops, and so concerns every gardener. Companion gardeners do not just ensure successful pollination by providing compatible partners; we also grow numerous companion plants to attract pollinating insects to the vicinity and to keep them there between different crops. Other plants are used to attract, feed and shelter predators or to repel pests. Companion gardeners aim to utilize and control weeds, not just to kill them, as weeds are some of the best plants for accumulating minerals generally in short supply and needed by our crops. They are grown as green manures and can be used to improve fertility at no cost and with little effort. Otherwise inaccessible nutrients can also be made available by growing the right companions whose roots have mycorrhizal bacteria and fungi extracting them from rock particles and the air.

The animal and plant microlife in the soil should be encouraged with the right companions not only because it improves the fertility, water-holding capacity and texture of the soil, but because most of these tiny organisms give off carbon dioxide, which plants need. The larger forms of life such as hedgehogs, birds and frogs should also be encouraged, with plants that provide them with food and shelter.

All forms of wildlife are valuable because of the carbon dioxide they produce, as well as the fertility and pest control they provide. Although carbon dioxide may contribute to the greenhouse effect if it reaches the higher atmosphere, it can do nothing but good in a garden. It is essential for plant growth and in short supply, even in cities, especially when the sun is shining strongly on still summer days. For this reason alone as many forms of life as possible should be encouraged to live in or visit your garden.

Of course people are among the animals sharing any garden. Whatever you believe about talking to plants for 'scientific' or other reasons, plants and people certainly interact. Plants are perhaps a little wiser than us, because no matter what anyone says to them, they take no notice. They only respond to our actions, and it is up to us to coax the best out of them by being good companions.

Some people are credited with having 'green fingers' or 'a green thumb' and everything they touch seems to burgeon with life. There may be some 'magic' at work in these cases, but almost anyone can produce good results with a little hard work and a lot of understanding. Plants are immediately responsive to changes in their environment and the other plants in the vicinity are among the most important factors in that

environment. People with green fingers may have a conscious or unconscious appreciation of their plants' interactions and what conditions each needs.

As companion gardeners we try to give each and every plant the best possible conditions from birth to table or compost heap. This includes: consideration of every other plant that is, has been or will be in the vicinity; the use of gentle, organic and biodynamic methods; and the introduction of many and various plants to foster and encourage the crops and the life in the soil and the garden.

If we succeed then the plants flourish, the garden throbs with life and crops thrive. Fruit and vegetables taste better, keep longer and make us healthy, while we do less and less work. What more could anyone want?

Chapter 1

Companion Planting in History and Mythology

The quotation from Virgil at the beginning of this book shows that companion planting dates back to antiquity. The old man plants not just food crops and utilitarian plants but flowers, and non-productive trees and shrubs; Virgil remarks on this because somehow the old man produces exceptionally well from land otherwise written off as useless.

Early references can be valuable, because although most people were illiterate two thousand years ago, they were probably as intelligent as we are and had far better memories and greater powers of observation. Also, less ecological damage had been done, so many plants and animals were common that do not exist today in any number, if at all.

The classical world had its own ecological disasters – northern Africa and southern Europe were forested until man wasted the soil and made deserts of them. Over-irrigation created salination problems in many once-fertile soils, while others were grazed down to rock. The Roman empire finally tumbled purely and simply because it could no longer feed its people from its own – or anyone else's – land.

Writers of the time travelled, exchanging and recording some horticultural practices but were often more interested in 'human interest' stories than in describing what to them was the everyday. Their views were complicated by beliefs involving whole pantheons of gods, demi-gods and spirits which had a direct hand in the workings of nature. Classical horticulture and agriculture were the pursuits of slaves – educated men merely supervised and, unfortunately, the practical, day-to-day affairs were not of as much interest as the accounts and returns. As a result, effort was put into increasing production without due regard to the long term, and soils became impoverished and eroded. Legislation was passed controlling the worst excesses and at one point prizes were offered for cures for ecological problems. Jays were officially encouraged, but even with legal backing they could make little impact on the recurrent plagues of locusts.

Although the ancients used some washes, they knew little else about combating disease. However, we can still pick up a few tips from them on natural pest control. Advice such as soaking seed in water before sowing or keeping it pest free in storage with leaves of cypress and laurel is still of benefit. Soda and olive oil made a soapy wash that would certainly kill aphids and weevils. Powdered earths and gypsum were effective as insect killers and tree-banding grease, made just as we make it today, protected against climbing pests. Burning sulphur was used to disinfect houses and is likely to have been employed in storage places if not in the garden. Gnats and mosquitos were driven away with burning resin and sheep were dipped, as they are today, in an unpleasant mixture, then of sulphur, pitch, fat, tar and extracts of squill and hellebore which is very likely to have been effective. An early method of riot control was burning darnel seed which gave off the classical equivalent of CS gas.

Many writers copied one another and few did any practical research, so some ludicrous ideas were handed on, but generally the ancients counselled good practices – even it they were nearly always from the point of view of the landlord! Columella lived at the same time as Virgil, in the first century BC, and wrote a twelve-volume book on agriculture which contains some interesting companion advice. He advocated interplanting cabbages, globe artichokes, lettuces and radishes with vetches, onions and wormwood: they would then not be troubled by pests, particularly caterpillars. He noticed that lupins suppressed weeds and remarked that elms were grown to support vines.

Varro, who lived two hundred years earlier, recorded that walnut trees made the ground sterile, oaks were detrimental to olive trees and vines did not do well near cabbages. Horace noted that elms and poplars were good grape supports and better than other trees. Cato suggested that cow dung sprays were effective against chewing pests and that caterpillars on cabbages could be destroyed with a tea of wormwood and houseleek.

Most prolific in his advice was Pliny the Elder, who lived in the first century AD. He was struck by the fact that wild trees were much more resistant to pests and diseases than cultivated ones. He associated the rust on wheat with rust on laurels; today we know that rust transfers between wheat and wild barberries, so 'laurel' may have been misobservation or misnomer. Pliny was aware of the competition for light, describing the way plants kill each other with thicknesses of leaves and by depriving each other of nourishment. He also wrote of plants putting out blends of scents or juices that were harmful to rivals. Turnips, he said, could be kept free of caterpillars by growing them with vetches and the same applied to cabbages with chick peas. Radishes and laurels were thought to be bad for vines. (Androcydes, doctor to Alexander the Great, recommended radishes as an antidote to excessive quantities of wine.) One most annoying snippet is that Pliny says birds can be kept out of fields of millet by planting a certain plant in the corners – it is a great misfortune that he doesn't tell us which plant!

Other classical ideas sound unlikely to work. Pliny seems to have had small faith in many, recording 'magic' rituals with little comment, but other writers reported what they heard with apparent conviction. It is hard for us to imagine how some of these beliefs ever came into being – why should sacrificing a red puppy on 25 April be thought to cure rust or mildew, or having a naked woman walk round the orchard ten times after lovemaking drive away caterpillars? Burying a toad in the middle of a field does not keep birds away any more than touching trees with the gallbladder of a green lizard protects them.

As the Roman empire faded, civilizations declined and the world looked back to a golden age, so writers were even more content to copy their

A wonderful old rose I took from a cutting grows bare low down, but that defect is hidden by the deliciously scented Clematis montana *'Wilsoni'.*

predecessors. The monastery gardens kept up much good gardening practice and saved many plants and herbs for medicinal use, but from the end of the classical era there was little fundamental advancement until the Renaissance. The development of printing and the introduction of plants from the New World combined to change gardening and agriculture more in a few years than it had changed in the previous thousand. The inhabitants of South America cultivated plants that were totally unknown in the Old World: maize, tomatoes, potatoes, sunflowers, most beans and many of the marrows and squashes, as well as different medicinal and ornamental flowers. They had been growing these as companion crops for centuries without damaging the soil and were supporting vast populations. De Soto saw beans growing with the other new crops of squashes and maize when he visited the Americas in 1539.

When these plants arrived in Europe they were initially little more than curiosities, but once accepted they became widely grown staple foods. We are indebted to those Andean Indians both for the crops and for the *Tagetes* marigolds they grew with them which have powerful companion effects. Ironically, along with these valuable New World plants there also came tobacco, which proved a more powerful and effective pest- and people-killer than most others of the time!

In Europe, various herbs were still in use as insecticides, especially for the house and body: hellebore, mustard, onions, rosemary, rue, squill, walnut, wild cucumber and wormwood all had a part to play. Most pests were controlled by hand and many may well have been eaten, especially in hard times – I can vouch for the fact that locusts are both tasty and nutritious (deep fried they taste a bit like prawns). Washes of oils, sulphur, soots and ashes were used but there are few records of companion planting as an aid to pest control. Gardens were primarily physics or herbaries where medicinal plants were cultivated; food was produced in the fields and orchards, and flowers grown purely for pleasure were rare. In his famous *Herball* (1597), Gerard noted that horseradish was not good for grapevines, but did not mention any other companion effects. Everyday agriculture was still largely based on Roman practices. However, in 1669, J. Worlidge wrote his *Systema Agricultura* and became one of the first ecologists when he recommended killing ants with arsenic and honey but safeguarding bees by putting this concoction in a box with but small holes.

With the Renaissance came geometric design and knot gardens, reflecting the imposition of man's order on nature, then the vast walled and heated gardens of the great houses with large workforces overcoming most problems by sheer force of manual labour and ever more noxious pesticides. Poisons containing lead, mercury and arsenic were used in increasing quantities in addition to the soaps and oily washes of the past. Meanwhile the small cottager grew his mixed plot more probably for convenience and from habit than with companion planting in mind.

Lord Townshend, experimenting in the eighteenth century and known to history as 'Turnip' Townshend, introduced four-fold rotation of crops, which greatly improved yields. The sequence of a grazed clover ley, wheat, a root crop, barley and then a ley again maintained fertility and minimized disease problems. At about the same time, Jethro Tull was studying the damaging effect weed competition had on yields; he invented the seed drill and combined its use with horse hoeing as a way of controlling weeds.

With these improvements came the enclosure of the commons. Small cottagers became poorer and a few families grabbed most of the land. Agriculture in Britain began to concentrate more on extensive production with bigger farms and fields and less on mixed and small-scale holdings.

In France, Parisian market gardeners intercropped successfully – with the aid of immense quantities of horse manure and labour they were growing four or five crops simultaneously. A typical mixture was cabbages, cauliflower, celery and lettuces in the open. Carrots, cauliflower, lettuces, radishes and turnips would be grown together under bell jars. Another combination was endives, onions, spinach, strawberries and turnips. A Monsieur Ponce is recorded as having sold 20,000 lbs of carrots, 20,000 lbs of onions and radishes, 6,000 head of cabbage, 3,000 head of cauliflower, 5,000 baskets of tomatoes, 5,000 baskets of choice fruits and 154,000 head of salad per annum from a 2.7-acre plot!

One of the first scientific works on pest control was by E. A. Ormerod, who collected information at the end of the nineteenth century. Although she placed complete reliance on existing cultivation methods and washes

Wormwood (Artemisia absinthium)*, seen flanking a cottage path, has long been regarded as an efficient pest deterrent.*

made from noxious household substances, a few interesting bits of information still escaped. Cabbages were less prone to damage from caterpillars when grown between celery trenches; carrot blossom moth could be lured on to parsnip flowers and potatoes used as a sacrificial crop to keep wireworms off hops. Ormerod observed that ladybirds were one of the best aphid eaters and also recorded blue tits and several other birds as being useful against pests. She considered weed competition an important problem and noticed that a number of weeds harboured pests between crops.

The Victorians believed that science could solve every problem. The low fertility of overcropped land was to be magically restored by adding the right powders. Soluble salts of simple chemical compounds were first used as fertilizers in small amounts on poor lands that were ill managed and this certainly improved yields. But by the time of the First World War research had shown that these chemicals could hardly substitute for dung manuring. Nevertheless, when the Second World War broke out only twenty-five years later chemical fertilizers had almost totally taken over from manure. Horses were replaced by petrol engines and their muck by white crystals also made from oil.

Agriculture, with gardening in tow, followed this chemical approach, regarding the soil as a fund of chemicals – the plants took them out and man put them back. This error made it necessary for more and more of these supposed fertilizers to be added each year in order to maintain production. Stronger pesticides then had constantly to be found to deal with the increasing pest problems caused by this malnourishment. Soon cocktails of chemicals were entering the soil, rivers, sea, air and our bodies.

And so it continued until the 1960s, with no real public awareness of the problems being created by the destruction and pollution of the environment. Rachel Carson's book *Silent Spring* (1962) was a watershed as people realized that even penguins in the Antarctic had become permeated with DDT.

Although this was the first time that the general public had become alarmed, a few people had been expressing concern since well before the Second World War. Soil scientists and agronomists had been horrified by the destruction of soils – the dustbowl crisis of the American Midwest in the 1930s, immortalized by John Steinbeck in *The Grapes of Wrath*, was only one of several stark warnings of impending catastrophe. It went largely unheeded by corporations, politicians and governments, but individuals were more concerned and many Americans began experimenting with gentler, sustainable methods of agriculture. Their investigations led them to most of the same conclusions as another movement started in Europe in 1924. Rudolf Steiner had been asked by a group of farmers to help them revitalize the poor soil they were working. The methods they devised are now known as biodynamics and place great emphasis on timing, rotation, companion plants and their applications for pest control and as green manures. Much of the work on companion effects has been done by biodynamic gardeners, mostly in continental Europe and the USA.

In Britain events took a slightly different path. In 1946 the Soil

Association was founded by people concerned about the danger to health from polluted and imbalanced food and the erosions and denudation of the top soil caused by changing farming practices. Their research led to emphasis on fostering the life in the soil as essential for producing healthy food and ensuring long-term sustainability. The methods they counselled were defined in the set of guidelines known as the Soil Association Standards and their system was described as organic.

There are a few differences between the theories followed by organic and biodynamic practitioners but their overall approach is very similar. Most of their handbooks, advice and methods are interchangeable, though the emphasis may be slightly altered. Obviously gardeners researching in the UK and Europe have more plants, pests and diseases in common with each other than with the USA. However, although a specific association or effect may be different, nature nearly always provides a parallel that fills the same niche, so we have much to gain by sharing our observations.

Perhaps the most prolific researcher into companion effects was Ehrenfried Pfeiffer.* He was one of the first to examine Steiner's suggestions and he developed them much further. His experiments showed how preparations made from certain plants could accelerate composting, encourage soil life and improve yields of various crops. He crystallized plant extracts which produced patterns that indicated whether or not those plants were companionable.

Current research is going on rather slowly: many gardeners are interested, but do not have the facilities to do much investigation. With a few honourable exceptions, mainly in continental Europe, business and government are not generally interested in the organic approach, and some are actively hostile. They are hardly going to investigate companion effects with no product to sell at the end of the day. The process of plant breeding has unwittingly eradicated or masked companion effects in many of our commercial plants and it is now illegal to sell non-EC approved varieties of most vegetables' seed. Soon fruit and flowering plants will be included in this ban and only commercial varieties will be legal. It is even an offence to grow non-standard varieties of some vegetables in some areas.

All of this handicaps companion practitioners. For example, thousands of varieties of oat were tested to see if they inhibited broad-leaved weeds from germinating. Only a few were found to do so. It is this lack of activity in most cultivars that prevents us discovering all the potential benefits offered by companion planting. If we are to make any progress, we must rediscover or rebreed species and varieties that have more active companion effects. Although individuals can achieve a certain amount by themselves, it is imperative that we influence the large institutions so that research is conducted on the vast scale that is necessary to save our productive land *and* to restore that which we have made desert.

*Pfeiffer's most interesting books are listed in the bibliography on p.172. Much of his work was assembled by Richard B. Gregg; this was added to by research on herbs by Evelyn Speiden Gregg and then by Helen Philbrick. First published in America, it was later revised for the UK by Joe Hill. Louise Riotte collated American information during the 1970s and in Germany Gertrud Franck has improved companion planting methods.

CHAPTER 2

UNDERSTANDING COMPANION PLANTING

The old lady, her cat and clover

Companion planting deals with very faint effects. But flowers keeping beneficial insects fed between crops are an intrinsic part of the garden, maintaining numerous predators and pollinators. Their effects may seem very small initially, but they add up over a period of time and show up most of all during difficult conditions.

Charles Darwin was well aware of these small effects. Although we remember him for his work on evolution, he was also fascinated by the humble earthworm and wrote a massive tome about it. He pointed out that although an individual worm contributed little to soil fertility, there were so many of them in an acre of land that in the course of a year they

Shasta daisies (Chrysanthemum maximum) *with lady's mantle* (Alchemilla mollis) *at their feet, seen over the flowers of rue. Sedum spectabile and goldenrod* (Solidago) *are still in bud, with flowers to come. Common tough plants form the backbone of these beds and over a period of several months provide continuity of flowers for beneficial insects.*

deposited 15 tons of animal droppings – as much as the best practice annual dressing of farmyard manure over a similar area. Darwin's research was wide-ranging and he was quick to realize that everything in nature was interconnected. In fact, he was one of the first writers to describe ecology as we now understand it.

He used to tell a story about the old lady, her cat and clover. He would explain that in a village with more than the average number of old ladies the grass had more clover and the meadows gave more hay. The reasoning behind this was a simple chain. Old ladies keep cats more than most people, so more old ladies lead to more cats in the village. These cats will roam the hedgerows and capture whatever they can, particularly field mice – so more cats, fewer mice. Mice are one of the few predators of wild bees' nests – so fewer mice, more bees. The bees are essential for the pollination of red clover – so more bees mean more clover. Clover improves the yield of hay – so more old ladies, more cats, fewer mice, more bees, more clover, more hay.

This is one of the basic lessons of ecology around which companion planting revolves, and it leads in turn to the blurring of some traditional boundaries. We are used to compartmentalizing our gardens into the flower garden, the herb garden, the vegetable patch, the orchard, and also subdividing the inhabitants of the garden into the wildlife, the livestock and the gardener. Companion planting insists that we adopt the holistic approach and see the garden not only as a whole, but as part of the local and world environment.

Dividing the garden up into distinct areas is often common sense for aesthetic and practical reasons, but for the best companion effects flowers and herbs need to be cultivated carefully amongst the vegetables and fruits, and vice versa. However, all this blurring need not complicate matters much – each area will still have its primary purpose, but with more plants mixed in than usual. Careful planning utilizes companion effects: putting the high trees of an orchard or a fruit cage on the windy side of a salad bed shelters it from harsh weather, while herbs planted with the salads attract beneficial insects.

Gardening practice needs little modification; it is more a question of a change of attitude. Weeds become a managed resource rather than a curse, as do pests such as wasps and even birds. Birds collect material from a wide area to feed their young and leave their excreta, shells, feathers and often bodies in the garden as high-value fertilizer. Their contribution to pest control is much more valuable than the cost of protecting fruit from their depredations. Bees do not just pollinate, giving honey and wax – they also drop down dead on the job, leaving little bits of fertility where they fall. Livestock is not just an egg- or meat-producer; it is also a fertility machine, converting low-grade waste into rich manure while devouring pests and breathing out that essential plant food, carbon dioxide. Even the worst pests are adding to the overall life of the garden – they may damage current yields, but will produce more in the long run as their waste products and eventually their bodies add fertility.

All of these various forms of life contribute material to the garden, as do the gardener and visitors, who can do a bit more quite easily. No matter how clever the system, it still loses many nutrients unnecessarily every time the WC is flushed. In my garden Personally Initiated Soil Stimulant diluted down twenty to one is used for activating compost or feeding grass, which is then cut as a mulch and fertility provider. This presents no health or hygiene problems, though I admit that solid waste is probably best treated conventionally.

Ecology is not a static event that can be pinned down; it is a continual interplay. Companion planting effects seem minor, but like the last snowflake they may cause an avalanche. Regular observation of natural processes and judicious action at the right moment can produce immense benefit later. Rubbing out buds that would grow in the wrong direction, spotting an infestation before it has spread or noticing a mineral deficiency are little things that can be tremendously beneficial if seen to promptly.

Putting the right plants together may not obviously produce much better results than haphazard mixing when other conditions are good. It is in poor conditions that the interaction of plant on plant or on other creatures is most noticeable, and then good results may justifiably be attributed to the gardener's skill.

This luxuriant growth was photographed in a hot, dry summer in the driest village in England, proving that the right plants in the right place will still do well in difficult conditions. Even the damp-loving hostas can flourish given partial shade from the yellow loosestrife. A foxtail lily (Eremus bungei) repeats the yellow background.

The mass of foliage and flowers underneath these roses keeps their roots cool and moist.

This is a crucial point – gardening skill *is* necessary. It is very important to put plants in the best place and give them the correct treatment. Any neglect or error here can far outweigh the benefits of most companion planting effects. Looking after the obvious needs will give satisfactory results in many seasons – it is when conditions are less than perfect that companion effects make all the difference between success and failure.

For example, if you cultivate early flowering fruits like apricots and peaches you may provide good growing conditions, but if the flowers are not pollinated the trees cannot fruit. As they flower early in the year there are few pollinators available and the weather conditions are often hostile to them. What pollinators there are will be concentrated in the area closest to their nests, so you will only have fruit if there is a nest nearby. These creatures site their nests in suitable places, not just for shelter but to be near food sources. Provide just a few of these and you will always have more pollinators about. Then in a difficult year, when many of these have perished during a hard winter and flowering comes in a cold damp period, your fruit will still be pollinated. If only one bumble bee in the area survives, it is all the more important to ensure that it is living in your garden and not anyone else's.

The importance of general skill, careful planning and good gardening practice cannot be overstated. Companion planting effects are important, but the basics must be right as well.

The table shows that plants may be good and/or bad companions for various reasons. These complex relationships become even more complicated when we consider all the other variables with their direct and indirect, negative and positive effects. For example, a tree may give off root secretions that are companionable to a plant and drop leaf exudations

THE DIFFERENT WAYS COMPANION PLANTING WORKS

1. Plants may help each other directly (providing shelter from wind and sun; root and leaf secretions; root channels).
2. Plants may help each other indirectly by improving the soil (mineral accumulators; green manures; humus and texture improvers).
3. Plants may compete with and/or directly harm others (competition as such; root and leaf secretions; replant disease).
4. Some plants help others if they are present in a small proportion, but hinder or harm them as the ratio increases.
5. Plants may repel harmful insects or attract them away from other plants (protective, camouflage, sacrificial and trap plants).
6. Plants may support insect populations which are beneficial to other plants (pollinators, predators and parasites to help pest control).
7. Plants may repel other and larger pests.
8. Plants may attract birds and other creatures which prey on pests and/or are generally beneficial.
9. Plants may reduce the incidence of fungal or other diseases in nearby plants.
10. Plants may be attractive and/or beneficial to animals and people.

that benefit it. The dead leaves may protect the plant's crown from frost and the tree's flowers may support a necessary pollinator. In turn, the plant may leave the soil about it enriched with minerals which the tree needs. But the shade will still kill the plant when the tree grows larger. Bear in mind that there is no altruism in nature – any good one plant does for another is coincidental from their point of view. However, we can utilize these effects for our own purposes and the plants may respond obligingly.

As we examine these different types of effect in more detail, remember that they are not independent. Many will be in conflict with each other, and there may be more interactions of which we are totally unaware.

How plants help each other directly

Shelter from wind and sun is one of the most obvious benefits plants can confer on each other. Windbreaks and hedges are important as they curb the worst excesses of the weather, but they also warm the garden by absorbing heat from the wind. Hedges reduce the wind's speed so that it extracts less water from the garden. As the wind slows down, it deposits any debris it is carrying, and this helps fertility.

In exactly the same way, established plants or the stumps of the previous crop create much better conditions for young seedlings and transplants. Shelter from the wind can allow predators and pollinators to work earlier in the year and for longer each day. Of course it is possible to overdo shelter and produce stagnant conditions or a frost pocket, but the worst problem likely to occur is reduced light from all the growth.

Some plants do need sheltering from full sun – shade lovers and new transplants in particular. For the most part plants prefer to be well exposed to the sun – after all, it is what makes them grow. But if you do have anything that needs protection, grow taller plants on the sunny side.

Many plants need cool, moist root runs, *Clematis* particularly so. A companion planting of leafy groundcover will provide conditions in which they can thrive. Spinach serves the same purpose in the vegetable garden, especially as it gets on well with almost everything.

Support can also play a part. Natural poles of sunflower or sweet corn can be grown for peas, ridge cucumbers, melons and marrows to clamber over. Sturdy shrubs and trees are the best framework for climbing roses, though more vigorous climbers like *Clematis montana* may tend to overwhelm their hosts.

Root channels are an invisible network that plants are continually expanding. During a plant's life the root hairs are continually replaced and once it is dead the larger roots start to decay as well. The pathways driven through the soil then become available to other plants as the decay proceeds, and are lined with nutrients from the breakdown. This is one reason why rotation and interplanting are important – a different type of plant will be better able to use these 'second hand' nutrients and run less risk of disease than if the same species is planted again in the same place.

Beneficial root, leaf and gaseous secretions are difficult to observe and they also vary enormously. The active part of any secretion is affected by

Shelter from this yew hedge protects a delicate Peruvian Alstroemeria.

weather, soil and season, but even more by the variety of plant. Plants are not all the same and even within a species there are many different cultivars. A cultivar may or may not produce the same companion effects as the species plant, especially if it has been highly bred for a particular purpose such as large flower size. You can hardly be blamed for failing to observe a recorded companion effect if the variety you are examining does not produce it!

A now dead plum tree makes a support for this 'Handel' rose; the peonies below could have done with more support for their big heads!

The variable effects of these secretions are inextricably tied up with the plants which aid each other through enriching the soil and those which aid in small amounts but hinder in large, so more will be said about these later (see below and p. 32). However, it should be noted here that many plants appear to have a beneficial effect on others independent of measurable soil enrichment, probably due to the recipient benefiting from byproducts discarded by the donor. For example, the root exudates of peas help other plants to absorb nutrients 'independently' of the nitrogen-fixing ability that peas and other legumes have.

Plants continually pass nutrients back and forth to their root hairs which are intermingled with the soil and replaced throughout the growing season. Their surfaces are coated and permeated by layers of the bacteria and fungi that coexist with them. Plants not only extract nutrients from the soil solution with the aid of this microlife, they also give them other nutrients in exchange. Often the microlife produces a surplus that is then available to other plants. Legumes are famous for this, as the nodules on their roots are very rich in nitrogen which has been 'fixed' from the air and is released when the root has been replaced, died and decomposed. Some plants, especially cereals such as barley, excrete potassium back into the soil as they ripen and most put unwanted materials into leaves that are about to be dropped. As all plants are in competition with each other, most secretions are used to deter other plants or pests (see p. 33).

How plants help each other indirectly by improving the soil

Soil improvement is done naturally but slowly by the succession of different plants growing on a piece of ground. Once the surface has been stabilized with a mat of mosses, grasses and shallow-rooting plants, deep-rooting plants like docks and thistles grow and leave pathways for tree and shrub roots to follow. We speed up the process by controlling the order, timing and selection of plants to suit the soil and situation. We may choose to improve the soil before planting a crop by digging in green manures, for example – or by growing certain plants simultaneously, as in orchards where alfalfa may be undersown. Undersown crops benefit in the autumn when the main crop is removed, leaving them to grow on and take up the breakdown products of the decaying roots and leaf litter.

If the soil is planted with different crops in rotation (companion planting over time), each crop is chosen to suit the conditions produced by the previous occupant and to leave those preferred by the following. Specific examples are given in Chapter 6 (see p. 130), but some plants are generally beneficial to the soil. Flax and *Phacelia* improve the tilth and bind together soil particles; spinach adds saponins which gel the humus with coarser organic materials, helping it to hold more water.

Leaf litter is another valuable soil food: plants use leaves they are about to shed as dumping grounds for unwanted minerals and byproducts, and these will feed the microlife and thus the crops. The amount of fertility introduced into the soil this way can be immense and can be increased by filling bare ground with cover crops that will trap wind-blown debris.

Soil enrichment may come either directly from plants leaving rotting root hairs and leaf litter or indirectly through them swelling the compost heap. The total quantity of fertility-producing plant material is increased by growing green manures as catch crops, intercrops and over winter. Introducing and encouraging the right plants to accumulate necessary nutrients improves the quality of the soil. The many weeds that concentrate scarce minerals are particularly useful in this respect .

Although weeds are competing to the death with our treasured plants, they are of immense value as mineral accumulators. As is explained more fully on p. 58, they are capable of extracting nutrients from soils that are extremely deficient in them, though this ability is not restricted to weeds. For example, the weed thornapple accumulates phosphates to nearly one third of its dry-matter mineral content, the leaves of the locust tree can similarly be three-quarters lime, and the potato accumulates magnesium. By digging in or composting these plants, we return this mineral wealth to the soil and make it available to the plants that follow. (See p. 157 for more examples of plants that accumulate specific minerals.)

Many companion plants get on well together because they root in different soil layers. This reduces one form of competition between them. The deep rooters bring up minerals from soil the shallower-growing plants cannot reach. The shallow rooters do not compete at those depths and their breakdown products will eventually wash down to feed the others.

Legumes are unique in making available the nutrient nitrogen their companion microlife fixes from the air. The legumes are a large family containing many garden plants, of which the most common are the clovers. The rhizobium bacteria in the clovers' roots are very efficient at fixing nitrogen; the surplus can then be used by other plants. A mixture of clovers is particularly useful and improves the yield of grass much more than a single variety does. Farmers used to grow cereals mixed with legumes and fed the mixed crop to animals, as separating the seed proved troublesome in pre-mechanized days. Trials have consistently shown that such a mixture of legumes and cereals can be considerably more productive than either or both grown alone. Peas and beans are equally beneficial in the vegetable garden and can be grown to advantage amongst many crops (see p. 138-139). Lupins, sweet peas and several trees including laburnum are also leguminous and are valuable in more ornamental areas.

Microlife enhancement is linked to soil enrichment, as plants such as yarrow and valerian which encourage worms and other creatures will enrich the soil in the process. An increase in the population of these animals means more byproducts and dead bodies to feed the crops. Improvements in the organic content, saponins and scarce nutrients in soil will encourage population explosions and thus multiply any inherent fertility the soil may have. Insect remains are of special value to the soil life, and chitin, the substance which forms their 'body armour', is believed to improve plants' resistance to disease.

Plants with sticky leaves, such as the alder and woodland tobacco *Nicotiana sylvestris*, or sticky stems, such as *Lychnis viscaria*, not only trap many insects to benefit the compost heap but can also thus be used for pest control.

Sweet peas are leguminous, so they enrich the soil for plants that come later.

HOW PLANTS COMPETE WITH AND/OR DIRECTLY HARM OTHERS

In the continual battle for air, light, water and nutrients plants use every method available to them to oust competitors. As mentioned above, root, leaf and gaseous secretions are either discarded byproducts or deliberately offensive chemical warfare. We can harness these effects, though it may lead to complications.

One early application of companion planting used wormwood to discourage cabbage butterflies; upon investigation it was discovered that the butterflies had indeed been discouraged, but that the wormwood had also washed off an exudation which reduced the growth of cabbages by between a quarter and a third! Clovers are inhibited by root secretions from buttercups and disappear where buttercups appear. This antipathy is so strong that an extract of buttercups diluted down to one part in twenty-three million still inhibits clovers. Clovers themselves give off secretions that inhibit other plants and even stop their own seed germinating at a dilution of three hundred parts per million.

Many plants give off ethylene gas, which prevents seeds germinating and affects the growth of other plants. It causes slower and therefore sturdier growth, which probably helps plants to resist wind and cling to supports. It also causes premature ripening, which may be advantageous to some crops. Dandelions give off more ethylene than most, but many plants emit it in response to gentle stroking.

The competition for nutrients and light is the main reason weeds have to be controlled. However, weeds can benefit other plants, not only by accumulating material for improving fertility, but also by acting as nurse crops, protecting small plants from the full force of the weather and hiding them from pests. But, to be quite frank, this useful effect is usually far outweighed by their damaging competition and their persistent harbouring of pests and diseases.

It is relatively easy to supply extra water, mineral nutrients and even freer air passage to compensate for competition, but it is difficult to supply more light. Severe shade is one of the main reasons for poor growth. Compound the problem with the dry conditions caused by overhanging boughs and few plants will prosper. Improving poor light is almost invariably beneficial and although some plants prefer light shade, the great majority do not. The exceptions are the shade-loving ornamentals such as skimmias, *Danae*, *Decaisnea*, hellebores and *Polygonatum*; saladings and leaf crops may also prefer shade during a hot summer. The canopy period is important – trees surrounding a garden are going to be detrimental if they come into leaf early and do not drop their leaves till late autumn. Trees such as ash which have short canopy periods are best.

Various plants are more adept than others at shading out their opposition. Taller plants have an obvious advantage, but the density and thickness of leaves can greatly affect the degree of shade. Oats and rye

These runner beans are not dense enough to shade out the herbs, and the saladings will appreciate the light shade on hot summer days.

increase their shading much faster than wheat, but neither is as effective as hemp. This once popular crop was grown for fibre and also because it was very efficient at smothering out weeds: from early on in its life it creates heavy, undiminished shade from ground level to over half its height. Unfortunately from this point of view, cultivating hemp is now illegal in most countries.

Tagetes minuta is a more usable smother crop which has even been known to suppress pernicious weeds like equisetum and bindweed. Its smothering effect is augmented by root secretions that inhibit herbaceous plants but have little effect on woody ones. These secretions also kill nematodes, minute parasitic worms which attack tomatoes and other crops. Chemical companies use such natural herbicides and insecticides as a starting place in their search for more powerful poisons. When you think of the vast numbers of plants they screen each year, you wonder what snippets of information they may have uncovered but never revealed!

Competition may be invisible under the ground, but climbers and strong shrubs will quickly and obviously monopolize light. They can exclude most of the sunlight from plants underneath, so be careful where you plant them. The same occurs on a smaller scale with carpets of creeping groundcover plants which prevent weeds from even starting. The dense shade provided by these plants can be used deliberately to inhibit weed germination, and groundcover is very useful in the ornamental garden. Dense growth, especially that of evergreens, suppresses weeds thoroughly. Conifers are often effective as their leaves/needles also inhibit seeds from germinating. Few seeds germinate under rosemary, wormwood or rue for the same reason.

In the productive garden close planting, block planting and intercropping with companion plants can exclude light from the soil and similarly handicap weeds. But beware of cramming too many plants in together – don't forget that although plants may not take up all the space above ground, there may not be enough room underground for all the root systems. Vegetables must have less competition in this respect than ornamentals.

The plants that grow most successfully despite summer shade are the spring bulbs – they come and go before the rest of the plants have stolen all the light and so are often easy to establish. They will not succeed under permanent shade, though.

Many plants compete by depriving others of essential nutrients if they can't shade them out. Those plants that start into growth earliest in the season can grab every bit of nutrient as it becomes available, so late developers are starved before they start. Perennials with massive food reserves in their roots have become expert at this method of beating the opposition. They use their reserves to grow before enough light is available for other plants and are thus able to take all the nutrients and light, leaving none for their competitors.

The elimination of nutrients is a factor in the effect known as 'replant disease', already mentioned. This is not really a disease as such; rather it is symptomatic bad growth which occurs when a plant is introduced close to where one of the same genus has recently been. Replant disease is worst

These tulips go wonderfully well with the magnolia flowers and their foliage gets plenty of sun before the magnolia comes into leaf.

for woody plants, especially roses and apples, but occurs to a lesser extent with most plants. Rice plants, for example, are known to inhibit their own offspring for the following year. Annuals and short-lived crops should be rotated to eliminate the problem. Trees are more difficult to rotate and if one dies or is blown down the temptation to put in an exact replacement must be resisted. In the vast majority of cases, if a replacement is the same genus as its predecessor, it will not thrive, no matter what you do.

Replant disease is due partly to the previous occupant having taken all the nutrients suited to the genus, partly to a build-up of pests and diseases, but frequently to residues of allelopathic compounds. Many plants suppress their own seeds from germinating underneath with these chemicals and others such as black walnuts (*Juglans nigra*) suppress almost everything. Allelopathic compounds will prevent a replacement plant from establishing itself for several years until they have broken down. By then the soil will have recovered its nutrient balance and the pests and diseases will have dissipated, making the site suitable once more.

How plants help others if they are in small proportion, but hinder or harm them as their number increases

Farmers have often noted that very small numbers of some weeds interplanted with crops increase yields and that some plants improve the quality of others nearby. If the proportion of these good companions increases, they start to compete with the crops and yields drop. The effect is probably due to hormones affecting the growth and nutrient uptake of the main planting. This is then overwhelmed by the depression in growth caused by the competition.

This phenomenon is particularly noticeable with cereals: yields of wheat are improved by very small numbers of corncockles, chamomile or white mustard plants, but larger numbers rapidly choke the crop.

Similarly, pungent herbs used as border plants aid the vegetables, but plant too many and competition sets in. Fennel, wormwood and rue may be better avoided altogether as they inhibit many plants. Stinging nettles pose another of these quandaries – they are hardly pleasant companions, but their presence makes fruit (particularly tomatoes) ripen fully with less rotting, and increases the oil content of herbs.

Lettuce and beetroot will be eaten by birds or slugs in preference to the sweet corn or squashes they surround and protect.

How plants repel harmful insects or attract them away from other plants

Plants can be used to aid others in many forms of pest control. A plant with a stronger odour may 'hide' another, or use leaf patterns or the 'wrong' flowers to camouflage it. Tomatoes next to beans deceive leaf hoppers, reducing the damage these cause. French beans or clover grown with brassicas have been shown to reduce aphid populations by 80 per cent, root fly attacks by 60 per cent and caterpillars by 33 per cent. Garlic and shallots reduce aphids, leaf hoppers and moth attacks on potatoes, but for some strange reason encourage thrips. The classic example is growing carrots and onions together to confuse their respective flies. (This is an effective control but not quite as good as isolating them with old net curtain.) Strong odours may not just mask crops – some, like that of the wormwoods, may drive the pests away altogether. Marigolds in the greenhouse deter whitefly, but will not drive them out once they are in.

Some plants have leaf or root exudations that make them distasteful to pests; these may transmit immunity to those growing with them by proximity or absorption. Nasturtiums are grown up through apple trees to drive away the woolly aphis; many people believe this to be effective, although it has not yet been proved in trials. Pungent herbs also bolster plants against pests. Sage brush has been shown to give off methyl jasmonate when attacked by insects: within a few hours this stimulated nearby tomato plants into manufacturing their own insect repellant.

You can lure pests away by planting 'trap crops' which are more attractive to the pest than the plants you want to protect: the idea is to entice the pests on to plants that will be destroyed or removed, taking the pests with them. Wireworms in new land can be attracted on to a mustard crop that is to be turned in, or on to a potato crop which will be dug up before the area is planted. Whitefly in the greenhouse are drawn to sweet tobacco plants which are then dispatched to the bonfire. Red spider mites cannot resist broad bean plants, but take longer to move on to them.

This sort of companionship is also known as sacrificial planting – the companion is sacrificed for the benefit of the valuable crop. An extreme case is growing strawberries to keep birds off gooseberries, if it is the gooseberries that you want to protect. Wild blackberries in the hedges will also reduce damage to other fruits in the autumn. Lettuce, spinach and other soft seedlings are eaten by slugs before tougher plants, so sow extra as sacrifices around the perimeter or shred a few and spread them around as easier, wilted snacks. Carrot blossom moths seem to go for parsnips in flower and leave the carrots.

Sacrificial crops are also of great benefit in breeding up predators to control pests elsewhere. This is particularly applicable to aphids, which have varieties that are specific to a very few plants, while the predators that feed on them do not usually mind what type of aphid they eat. Growing more honeysuckles, lupins and cherries that regularly get covered in aphids is not going to infect many other plants, but the ladybirds and other predators bred up on these aphids will eat wherever they can, controlling the pests on your more valued plants.

HOW PLANTS SUPPORT INSECT POPULATIONS WHICH ARE BENEFICIAL TO OTHER PLANTS

Increasing the numbers of pollinators, predators and parasites in the garden is not just a means of helping pest control. Every form of life eventually becomes a food resource for some other creature. All these chains of life are concentrating nutrients and depositing them as byproducts and dead bodies which build up the general level of fertility. A bees' nest may contain 50,000 bees at midsummer; although the colony may survive for some years, none of the individual workers were alive last year and none will be next. They are continually being replaced, so a single nest can drop 50–100,000 dead bees in the surrounding area in a year and each adds an extra drop of fertility.

   Some plants are especially good at attracting and feeding beneficial insects, so growing them will rapidly increase the populations of these allies. Among the best are buckwheat (*Fagopyrum*), poached egg plant (*Limnanthes douglasii*), alpine strawberries, *Convolvulus tricolor* and *Phacelia tanacetifolia*.

Probably the best companion to roses, shrubs and soft fruit is Limanthes douglasii, *a self-sowing annual, here shown under my gooseberries.*

Many flowering plants attract hoverflies and bees, but often different ones appeal to butterflies and moths. Bees see in the ultraviolet spectrum and mainly prefer flat flowers with bluish colours. Butterflies are guided more by scent and pheromones than by sight, so colour is less important, but they seem generally to prefer orange and red shades with deep tubular flowers. A wide range of plants will bring in and encourage many and various pollinators, beetles and flies as well as bees and butterflies.

Different predators and parasites can be attracted in the same way. The aim is to provide a staggering diversity of food (flowers and pests) and shelter over as long a season as possible so that there are always plenty of useful insects about.

HOW PLANTS REPEL OTHER AND LARGER PESTS

Thorny or prickly plants are excellent deterrents which can be useful for discouraging cats and dogs from fouling the soil; on the other hand, they may annoy people, so be careful where you let them grow.

Some plants give off smells that are repulsive to animals: dwarf elder and elder leaves are said to discourage mice; rabbits are supposed to dislike onions; and root exudations from euphorbias are an ever-hopeful *possibility* for a reliable mole deterrent. Pungent herbs and leaves with strong secretions such as wormwood can be used to discourage slugs and snails.

Unfortunately, apart from the direct physical action of thorns and the terminal effects of poisonous plants, few plants have any really practical applications as forms of animal control. Hungry or mischievous creatures are only going to be stopped by mechanical barriers.

HOW PLANTS ATTRACT PREDATORS, BIRDS AND OTHER CREATURES

Although birds do a lot of damage to crops, their overall effect is beneficial – they control pests, concentrate fertility and generally add life to the garden. Encourage them with plants offering perches, shelter and food. By having as many different plants as possible supplying fruits and berries over as long a season as possible, you will attract a variety of birds which are both useful and enjoyable to watch and listen to.

Any plants creating dense shelter will attract hedgehogs, and others giving cool moist shade can encourage frogs, toads, newts and slow-worms. All these creatures eat pests, though to be honest they will also eat useful predators that are too slow to escape.

HOW PLANTS REDUCE THE INCIDENCE OF FUNGAL OR OTHER PLANT DISEASES

As fungi are actually just another form of plant life they might be included under the heading 'How plants compete with and/or directly harm others', above. However, as fungi do not use photosynthesis it is worth considering them separately. Most fungi are saprophytic, which means

A bench and planter transform this warm corner. In the planter are marguerites or Paris daisies (Chrysanthemum frutescens), *which need to be taken under cover for overwintering.*

Wormwood and foxgloves contain powerful poisons, but some plants will flourish near them.

they live on dead matter that they decompose, but many also attack living plants and creatures. Bacteria also most often feed on dead material, but plenty of varieties attack living cells too.

Many root exudations and plant secretions act as chemical warfare against these attackers, which in turn use other chemicals to gain entry to plant cells. Fungi use their own secretions to attack and destroy bacteria. Penicillin and most of our other antibiotics have been developed from research into these chemicals.

Plants which are rich in silica offer some benefit and sprays made from garlic, stinging nettles and equisetum have proved useful. When a green manure of flax or mustard breaks down in the soil it releases cyanide gas and related compounds in minute amounts; this kills *Fusarium*, *Helminthosporum* and *Verticillium* – which are undesirable – while leaving useful fungi such as *Trichoderma*, *Mucor* and *Penicillum*. Many green manurings with seedling mustard may also help decrease brassica clubroot infections from old cabbage plots. Dandelions exude cichoric acid from their roots and this has been shown to control *Fusarium* wilt disease in tomatoes. Charlock, a pernicious weed, secretes chemicals that destroy both fungi and eelworms.

Apart from specific examples like these, we know little about how different plants aid others against disease, except that anything that promotes plant health is naturally going to help prevent disease. Plants observed to be good companions may just be exhibiting this very effect. But simply because our knowledge is still so limited, this area of companion planting is the most potentially exciting.

How plants attract and/or benefit animals and people

Food plants are obviously useful, but here we are referring to aesthetic effects such as beauty and scent, and to medicinal benefits. Many plants are a delight to our senses and it would be arrogant to believe that other animals cannot appreciate them as well. A beautiful plant or a wonderful scent can be of immense benefit to the gardener and friends. Pleasant surroundings are very good for restoring physical and mental health and, after all, most gardens are primarily for our enjoyment.

As with all things, beauty in the garden is very much in the eye of the beholder, and only you can choose plants which please you. However, many plants, especially herbs, are attractive to animals for medicinal reasons. Natural medicines occur in a wide variety of plants – over half our medicines are still based on plant products. Animals seem instinctively to find the right plants to cure themselves. They can sometimes be as stupid as us, though, as if a cow eats something that makes it ill it is perfectly capable of going back and eating some more!

Some of the complex companionships nature can create

The companion approach recognizes that everything is interconnected: the predator is absolutely dependent on the prey and benefits it by eliminating the sick and infirm and preventing it from exhausting its own food supply. Any alteration in the prey's food supply also affects the predator, which in turn affects any creature that preys on the predator, and so on ad infinitum. Nature designs an amazingly intricate weave of checks and balances which prevents any species predominating for long and ensures that every niche which can support life is utilized. Nature also strives continually to produce more life and more diversity; our aim as companion gardeners is to adjust the balance in our favour. Just how complex nature can be is illustrated by some of the different forms of partnership she has created and the varying levels of interdependence that result.

Parasitism is the arrangement whereby one partner gains everything and the other nothing. Mistletoe is a fair example: it is totally dependent for its survival on the few trees that make suitable hosts, which do not benefit at all from its presence. What goes unseen is the other partnership in the mistletoe's life, with birds that transport its seed – some species have evolved digestive tracts specially adapted to deal with mistletoe berries. One bird passes the seeds through four to twelve minutes after feeding and in so doing will spread them out along the length of a branch.

Some parasites start out being harmless to their host, but eventually do it some damage. Ivies and certain climbers only use other plants for support, but may compete to such an extent that they choke them out. Dodders and broomrapes are much more greedy than mistletoe and consume nearly all of the host plant's sap.

All these herbs and many more have long been used for their medicinal effects and are still the source of many modern drugs: comfrey, angelica, sweet cicely and rosemary are among those shown here.

Parasitic plants may have others preying on them – there are many cases of three, four or more parasitic plants existing in a chain, often with various fungi attacking them as well.

Commensualism means that one plant lives in, on or with another with no harm or benefit to either side: orchids and ferns live on trees in this way, for example.

Mutualism occurs when both sides gain from each other. Many such cases involve insects – ants living inside trees and protecting those trees from attack by other insects, for example. Butterflies mate by scent, which is the same as the scent of the flowers they are associated with, and they pollinate these flowers in return for nectar. Arums have a heated spathe in the flower that not only attracts pollinating insects but warms them up so that they can fly further afterwards.

Symbiosis is an even closer relationship in which both are inextricably joined in a fine balance; the vast numbers of associations between nitrogen-fixing bacteria and plant roots are examples. Lichens are the combination of primitive plants that have joined up symbiotically with fungi to create forms of life different from either that can live in conditions neither would survive alone. In most cases they exchange nutrients to mutual benefit. Some plants are limited to one partner, but Scots pines have up to 120 different fungus partners.

HOW THE ORGANIC METHOD ENHANCES LIFE

Organic methods mean guarding and encouraging the life in the soil, and the possible use of any chemical or spray is assessed with this in mind. Obviously we do not allow things that are harmful to people or that despoil the environment, but we object to the *effect* a substance has, rather than to the substance itself. Organic gardeners disapprove of most chemicals not simply because they are chemicals but because they damage life. *All* herbicides are forbidden, therefore, as they destroy not just the obvious plants but also the algae and microscopic forms of life. Most fungicides are banned because they do not stop working when they hit the soil, but kill valuable fungi there as well as the unwanted fungi they are meant to control.

Insecticides are often indiscriminate, killing friends as well as foes; they are also the group of pesticides with the worst history of side effects and damage to the environment and to people. They can have side effects for the crops, too. One large greenhouse market-gardening company converted to biological controls in preference to insecticides and their yields went up by between 14 and 20 per cent.

Guano (petrified seagull droppings) is as natural a fertilizer as you can get, but it is no longer allowed under the organic standards because its effect on soil life is deemed to be detrimental. However, it is only the concentrated substance that is harmful; in very dilute solution it is of benefit. The same applies to soluble fertilizers that come as crystals or

Supports can be grown 'in place': long cuttings of willow will root and can then be trained as frames or poles.

powders – the problem is with the concentration. To use an analogy, I am rather fond of good wine and a single glass with each meal can only be of benefit. But if I extracted the alcohol from each glass and then took a fortnight's worth in one gulp it would probably kill me. The same principle applies to soluble fertilizers. They are a convenience food when used the way houseplants are fed, with a very few crystals diluted in a gallon of water. Add too much fertilizer and the houseplants die in just the same way as the grass turns brown if you put on too much lawn feed.

The benefits of soluble fertilizer are that it supplies much needed nutrients in a rapidly accessible form and is cheap in terms of cash and labour. The drawbacks are that it pollutes water and the environment, and that scarce resources are depleted in order to make it in the first place.

The danger of soluble fertilizer is two-pronged: first, it extracts water from the surrounding soil and living cells so that it can become a solution, but it kills them in the process. Then it changes the balance of life in the soil, favouring the wrong organisms: the fertility-producing forms are displaced and the organic matter in the soil is broken down by others, giving a temporary boost to fertility that is soon over.

The depletion of organic material by excessive fertilizer use then lessens the water-holding capacity of the soil and the level of life decreases, requiring the use of yet more fertilizer. The plants are thus subjected to greater water stress during dry periods, while in good conditions the lush soft growth is easily attacked and penetrated.

The concern of the organic gardener not to damage soil life means that soluble fertilizers cannot continue to be used. If you have soluble fertilizer you want to dispose of, the least harmful method is to dilute it down so that it is weaker than standard houseplant feed and then to water it occasionally on to grassed areas. In this very dilute solution it will do no harm and will be converted into grass clippings for use elsewhere.

High nitrate levels may be directly harmful to our health, but tests show that more problems occur in the long term, as soluble fertilizers displace vital elements from the food they produce. As early as the Second World War it was noted that although production of blackcurrants was doubled by increased fertilizer input, vitamin content decreased in almost direct proportion. Smaller potato tubers have higher concentrations of Vitamin C, slower-growing leaves contain more than faster-growing ones. The effect is similar even when natural manures are used, although it is rather more difficult to apply these in really excessive amounts as they are so much more dilute already.

As an alternative to chemical fertilizers, we must build up fertility from the soil itself. This means growing plants specifically to be turned into compost with the addition of weeds, animal waste, household waste, ground rocks and seaweed products. An amazing series of population explosions occurs in the compost heap as different forms of life break down the material, more life lives on these and it in turn becomes prey for other creatures. The compost becomes a pile of myriad forms of life made up of dead bodies, their excreta, half broken-down material and humus.

When this is put into the soil it starts a similar process there and the dead bodies and excreta produced then feed the plants. The same happens when we add green manures directly – rock dusts or bonemeal, for instance. Micro-organisms that could not reproduce because phosphate was short will start to eat the bonemeal; their numbers increase, their predators flourish and that starts off another chain. As chains interact with each other to form yet more chains, the total amount of life in the soil escalates. The plants absorb nutrients through incredibly fine root hairs that penetrate almost everywhere and are continually being renewed and replaced. The surfaces of these roots are covered in bacteria and fungi that live in harmony with the plant and they gain mutual benefit swapping nutrients they extract from the soup around them. The healthier and more active all this life is, the more fertile the soil will be, and we can garden successfully knowing that we are doing nothing in any way destructive to the environment.

CHAPTER 3

HOW PLANTS HAVE BECOME COMPANIONS

The cultivars that go together to make up our gardens have been selected in many ways from an immensely larger number of potential or unlikely plants, sometimes deliberately but more often by chance. New plants with or without some obvious utility are still being discovered today, but the vast majority were recorded and catalogued by the end of the last century and many have been with us since the days of the Roman empire.

The course of evolution inevitably produced some edible or useful plants from the great multitude that were suited to cultivation. Hunter-gatherers, dropping unwanted seeds and rotting fruits, later found their food crops growing nearby as if by magic. Over the centuries these chance events were formalized and agriculture developed.

Geranium *'Ann Folkard'* and Heuchera micrantha *are hardy plants which do well in the same sunny spot. The feathery effect of the heuchera makes a pleasing background to the geranium's striking magenta flowers and bold foliage.*

Initially, plants would have been selected for yield, colour or usefulness; their size, physical form and nature dictated how they must be treated, so only some survived primitive methods of cultivation. There are countless plants that might have developed into crops but never got started. For example, we never improved elderberries – they are edible, but not tasty, and they are full of seeds. The bushes are easy to grow and produce lots of fruit, yet we have not selected or bred a larger-berried version. Mahonias, fuchsias and amelanchiers with their edible fruits are other possibilities we have passed by.

Centuries of cultivation have continually altered the candidates that were originally most suitable, almost beyond recognition in some cases. For example, grapevines are dioecious in the wild – that is, they have separate male and female forms – but selection, probably unconsciously, has produced modern cultivars which have both sexes on the same vine. No close relatives of bananas, maize or dates survive in the wild, as the cultivated forms have supplanted them. Cultivated brassicas are very different to the related wild coleworts and slowly revert if left to themselves. Rosemary has become hardier over many years, and celery used to be bitter. The centuries of cultivation have similarly selected and altered our weeds, pests and diseases, and their parasites and predators have adapted in their turn to create our current garden ecology.

All the whims and vagaries of fashion, accidents of history, varying soils and climates have contributed to reducing the vast numbers of possible plants to those we are able to choose from today. However, the choice still runs into many tens of thousands of different cultivars for food crops and even more for ornamental plants.

Gardeners have found it practical to split this multitude into more manageable groups *that tend to get on well together*. The short-lived, small-scale food crops are lumped together as vegetables and grown in one area. The woody plants cultivated for their flowers or aesthetic appeal are used to form shrub borders. Non-woody ornamental plants make up the herbaceous border and woody food plants are confined to the fruit cage or orchard.

These groupings may sometimes be nominal, purely for convenience, but mostly they show important relationships that exist between certain plants. The majority of plants in each grouping have a lot in common, and prefer similar treatment and conditions. Moreover, many of them have been selected and grown together in these groupings for as long as they have been known. Centuries of practical experiment and observation have taught which plants will get on with one another, and any 'anti-social' plants will rapidly have been evicted or placed away from the rest.

So companion plants already exist all round our gardens, as over time only those that do get on with the others have been propagated. These groupings of plants continue to consolidate, as most of the plants concerned not only prefer the same conditions but are selected and adapted so that they continue to do so. More often than not we use these groupings from habit rather than consciously: vegetables are not put in the

This glorious old lilac may be drab out of season, but its scent now is intoxicating.

shrub border, less because we recognize that most of them would not flourish there than out of convention. Introducing food plants into the flower garden is enjoying a revival in fashion, but this rarely proves satisfactory. Although it is part of the philosophy of companion planting to reduce monocultures and increase the diversity of plants, this only works if their individual needs are met. Most vegetables just will not prosper amongst such diverse and efficient competitors as you find in a mixed border. If you want more variety in the border, fruit trees, herbs and berries are a better bet.

Now I am not maintaining that it is impossible to make a 'flower' garden that is primarily aesthetic *and also* productive. What I am saying it that it must be planned as such from the start. The choice of crops will be slightly limited and 'all the year round interest' difficult to maintain, but good planning can help compensate. What cannot be done successfully is introducing most food crops into an established 'flower' garden – they will not 'do'.

PLANTS ASSOCIATED BY HISTORY

The plants that make up our gardens have been handed down to us from our ancestors and we should be grateful for all the care and work that went into their selection and development. Many plants have become very different from the original wild species not only in yield and appearance but in flowering time, pollination and cultural requirements. Characteristics such as pest- and disease-resistance may have been lost or enhanced. Our relatively recent reliance on chemical crutches may have led to the elimination of natural resistance in some plants. This can happen even with old varieties that originally had a useful companion effect – the seedsman rogues out different plants, but is only concerned with the 'important' factors such as yield or colour.

Companion gardeners should be careful when choosing highly bred cultivars in case the very effect they wish to use has inadvertently been lost. If marigolds fail to deter whitefly, it may be because you are using a variety that does not have exactly the right scent. For marigolds to be effective requires the pungency that some people object to, and this may have been altered while selecting for flower colour or dwarfism.

F1 varieties are the first generation offspring of the combination of two inbred lines. This gives them hybrid vigour and uniform characteristics, but may simultaneously eliminate other useful traits. They frequently have another great handicap for the household producer. Most seed is bred for agricultural use, not for gardeners. Agricultural varieties are chosen so that the crop matures simultaneously across a huge area and harvest by machine is possible. Gardeners may prefer to use non-F1 or older versions that produce crops over a longer period. After all, what good are two dozen cauliflowers ready together? Using a non-F1 variety can spread the same harvest over at least two or three weeks – much more practical for domestic purposes.

A further disadvantage (to the user) of F1 seed is that it does not work very well if you save your own seed. The breeder will have crossed two different strains to give a known result, but the resultant hybrid can then only give variable seed. To use a familiar analogy, mules are produced by crossing a donkey with a horse, but are themselves sterile; most F1s are not sterile, but they will not come 'true'.

The likelihood of losing a useful companion gene increases if the crop is cross-pollinated. Most cereals and legumes are self-pollinated and not easily variable, so they are likely to retain unknown genes controlling companion effects. Rye, maize, grasses, beet, carrots, brassicas and spinach are cross-pollinated and therefore more variable; companion effects are unlikely to exist actively in many varieties, though the gene may endure inactively and recur spasmodically.

If plants are propagated vegetatively, as many of our garden flowers, shrubs and most of our fruits are, then each plant is a clone, an exact replica of the original – it will therefore also have the original's companion effects. Many old varieties of flowers and particularly fruits and vegetables have disappeared beyond recovery – for one reason or another they became unpopular or were unsuccessful, so people stopped growing them and they died out. Once they are gone it is almost impossible to recreate them, and we should preserve different varieties of any plant in case they have unknown valuable attributes. Seeds can be stored indefinitely with occasional replenishment, but plants that are propagated vegetatively cannot be kept alive except as growing plants.

A Bramley's seedling is not just a graft on new roots, it is a bit of the original apple tree still growing ever onwards. Unless it has mutated it is a clone, exactly the same tree with all its original idiosyncrasies, although these may be slightly modified by different soil or rootstock. The fruit in your garden today will not vary enormously from the fruit on the original tree of Bramley's seedling at Southwell, Nottinghamshire, where it was first found nearly two hundred years ago.

The pests and diseases associated with an original interact similarly with subsequent clones, so to survive for long any cultivar must be pretty tough. But problems, especially viruses, can be difficult to eradicate from grafted and suckered plants. As each plant is a piece of the original given new roots, any infection carries on through each propagation. Grafted plants also need watching to make sure the rootstock does not become a bad companion, replacing the chosen cultivar with shoots or suckers. As most rootstocks are propagated by suckering, the suckers must always be removed as they steal nutrients from the rest.

Fashion, economics and climate all affect the survival of plants, so any that endure must have really outstanding qualities. Some old varieties have probably come down to us unchanged from Roman times, like the apple Court pendu plat and common asparagus. In these instances, the virtues of the original plant are so great that newer versions have not replaced them, but many once legendary cultivars have been lost. There are nurserymen's lists of apple varieties running into thousands, gooseberries in over a hundred different sizes and colours, but now you would be hard pressed to find more than two or three. The vegetables we grow are predominantly newer and newer varieties, as anyone reading a seed list of Victorian times will notice. Few indeed are the survivors from before

1840, but these have proved themselves for over 150 years! Green Windsor broad beans, now a favourite for freezing, were first sold in 1809, the year the Bramley apple was introduced. Red Drumhead cabbage has been sown for pickling, cooking and salads, summer and winter since 1835. All of these look young when compared to Ribston Pippin apples, excellent for winter use with one of the highest Vitamin C contents – they have been in our gardens since 1707.

Of course some relative newcomers can become weeds and be everywhere very quickly: it is astounding to note that *Buddleia davidii*, which grows on almost any bit of dirt in most cities, has only been known in Britain since 1890.

Some people may despise certain plants because they are common, complaining they are seen everywhere. What better testimony could they get? Take forsythia: like other common plants, it is easy to grow on most soils, tough as old boots, and has packed colour into cold, bleak spring days every year since Queen Victoria was a girl. Plants may disappear despite being popular, however: Laxton's Superb pear has gone as it harboured fireblight. *Berberis* is eradicated in most of the US to protect wheat from rust and currants are likewise banned, supposedly to save white pines, an important timber tree.

The plants that have persisted as garden cultivars for the longest have been continually reselected, but some old favourites are replaced and then reintroduced later. Gardener's Delight tomatoes and Pink Fir Apple potatoes are Victorian versions that have recently been 'discovered'. Old roses continually make comebacks despite the fact that many are poor flowerers. However, it is among these earlier varieties that we should look for the best companion effects. They were selected because they did well, while plants that were easily upset or obviously detrimental to others were

Opposite: Laxton's Superb, a wonderful apple enjoyed every year since it was introduced in 1822.

Two glorious old roses – Rosa 'Adelaide d'Orléans' (left) and R. 'Ballerina'.

eliminated. Varieties introduced since have been more scientifically bred, so there is less hope of them retaining many companion effects.

In the same way that most garden plants have been chosen mainly because they survive our conditions (few gardeners keep growing anything that fails consistently), weeds have survived simply because they are so good at it, despite all our attempts to eliminate them. We have also often introduced garden plants which turned into weeds and these now go unnoticed. Sycamores are a recent introduction and have most definitely become weeds. The Romans have been blamed for introducing nettles into the UK, and the rosebay willow herb is said to have been spread from trackside gardens by the early trains. Goutweed or ground elder was certainly brought here by the Romans and probably horseradish as well. Equisetum or marestails was cultivated to make pot scourers.

The way we have weeded our fields and gardens in the past has selected our present weeds. The process continues – as combine harvesters push everything except the wheat grains out the back, they sow the next crop of weeds. This selects for those that are ripe at the same time, of a different seed size to wheat and tall enough to be cut. Thus it is only to be expected that wild oats should be a problem, made worse because they are closely related to cereal crops and are spared by weedkillers.

Digging deeply brings up long-lived seeds to flourish again: the fields of Flanders turned red with poppies, but you can be sure there were also charlock, nightshades and knotweeds in profusion. In the garden, weeding done at long intervals has favoured weeds that germinate, grow and set seed quickly. Over many generations of this unconscious selection we have speeded up the reproductive process of our weeds. Some, like annual meadow grass and hairy bitter cress, can have a new generation every six weeks in good conditions.

Good gardeners recognize this historical selection process and use various methods to break it. In the vegetable plot rotation changes the prevailing conditions and the weeds most suited to those conditions change as a result – this regular annual upheaval prevents any type of weed being favoured long enough to become a problem, though any plant that is suited to many differing conditions will almost automatically become a weed however much rotating you do. Weeding at more frequent intervals stops the build-up of short-lived weeds and eradicates perennials. Mulching with loose materials makes weeding easier and keeping the soil filled with groundcover, crops or beneficial plants will prevent weeds from gaining a foothold.

PLANTS ASSOCIATED BY BIRTH

During the Renaissance horticulturalists thought that if they brought orange and lemon trees northwards very slowly they would gradually acclimatize to the harsher conditions. The trees cannot adapt, in fact, but sowing seeds from those that survived furthest north would work slowly with each generation. A rapid change can only occur if a mutation or some hybrid cross has produced a genetic difference. Woody plants were mostly propagated vegetatively by cuttings and this changed plants very little;

Wild red poppies are very quick to colonize newly exposed soil. We have learned to use this ability to fill gaps in our planting schemes with the prettier selected form, the Shirley poppies.

improvements only came as slight modifications from chance sports or mutations. Most other plants were grown from seed and there was no systematic breeding for improvement until Mendel started experimenting with peas in the nineteenth century. Selection was done empirically; seed was saved, hopefully from the best plants, without manipulating their pollination. Although there was some inadvertent hybridization, gardeners would automatically have selected for disease-resistance and possibly beneficial companion effects.

From the Victorian period onwards scientific breeding took over. New varieties of almost every plant were introduced as they were hybridized with distant relatives. Crossing a common garden form with a rare or an unusual species meant new colours or other characteristics could be acquired. Hybrids between species also tended to be more vigorous, so many crosses and recrosses were tried with almost every genus. In all this sudden and extraordinary mixing of varieties, many plants may have gained or lost the very genes that gave them companion and other beneficial effects. For example, potato plants used to be very hairy and this deterred aphids and other pests. The hairiness disappeared, probably as part of a deliberate policy, as it would have made the plants more prone to disease in wet conditions. Now that very quality is being re-introduced from wild Andean potatoes. Lloyd George raspberries were unpalatable to aphids, so they rarely succumbed to the viral diseases those creatures spread. None of the more prolific varieties of raspberry bred to replace Lloyd George have the same degree of immunity, presumably because of an oversight on somebody's part.

Despite the possibilities of genetic manipulation, our plants are still recognizable and known by their parenthood. In the eighteenth century, the Swedish scientist Linnaeus started the Latin naming of plants and in his system most are grouped according to the formation of their flowers. Linnaeus was lucky, as it would seem that flowers are a good indicator of evolutionary lines, so matching plants by flower type does usually create groups of closely related plants. For example, those with a flower like a rose are known as Rosaceae; this family includes most of the top fruit such as apples and pears, and many garden favourites such as *Crataegus*, *Sorbus*, *Potentilla* and *Geum*. Most Rosaceae are shrubby or tree-like and only a few are herbaceous. It is not difficult to see how they resemble one another and have evolved from a common predecessor.

The genus of a plant is more important to the practical gardener than its family – after all, roses differ quite a bit from apples, although both are Rosaceae. The general form of the family remains in the flower and leaf, but different parts became specialized as each version adapted to specific conditions. Roses are suited to woodland edge and clamber over lower growths with the aid of their thorns, while apples have opted to become trees – much like pears, but also very different.

As a general rule, all species of a genus resemble each other in many more ways than they resemble other genera, but they may or may not *look* similar, the differences being mainly botanical. Apple (*Malus*) and pear (*Pyrus*) trees look much the same and belong to the same family as plums (*Prunus*), which they resemble less. Examination of the buds, flowers, fruit

Aphids and other pests searching for this apple tree are confused by the scent of chives, thyme and southernwood growing underneath. (The aquilegia seedling is just a pretty opportunist.)

and bark shows up more differences and similarities than a casual glance reveals. Most apple trees resemble each other far more than they do pears or plums, but there are always those on the margin which are less distinguishable. These often closely resemble the wild varieties, as our selection process is continually causing a greater divergence. Any original companion effect is most likely to be retained in the more primitive forms.

Pests are commonly confined to a specific genus, though some may be less discriminating. Aphids are widespread, but each type may be very particular about what it will feed on and will not often move from one genus of plant to another except seasonally. Many aphids swap hosts for the winter months: one sort of black aphis prefers broad beans in the spring and summer but overwinters on spindle bushes. The maggots that attack apples do not attack pears and are different again on plums. Most diseases are also predominantly genus specific – silver leaf disease is

Because roses are grown so widely, they are prone to many pests and diseases, particularly aphids and blackspot. Companion planting will deter most pests, while tending your plants carefully should mean you notice signs of disease before they spread too far. The roses in this pretty bower are R. 'Goldfinch' and R. 'Mme Plantier'.

normally confined to members of the *Prunus* genus, for example. Fireblight is an exception and attacks almost all woody Rosaceae.

The soil and cultural requirements also vary more from genus to genus than within each one. Every genus is most suited to certain general conditions and although an individual species may have its own particular requirements, these will normally fall within the confines of those general parameters. Apples all like much the same conditions and these are almost but not quite good enough for pears, which need a slightly richer, moister soil and a bit more warmth and shelter.

There are very many more families in the flower garden than in the productive areas, but often only a few species of a single genus will be represented. *Acanthus* and *Euphorbia* are examples; rue is another 'orphan', the only member of the large Rutaceae family we cultivate. Some families are more widespread: the pea-flowered Leguminosae are not restricted to peas and beans but include such diverse genera as lupins, the brooms and laburnum. Even the tree members of this large family can have the ability to fix nitrogen, so they are frequently good companions.

The Solanaceae are mainly the potato and tomato family but also include the nightshade weeds and a pretty climber *Solanum crispum* 'Glasnevin'. Although the leaves and stems are full of poisonous alkaloids, as are green potatoes, this does not stop all pests attacking them. Tomatoes are so

*The potato vine (*Solanum jasminoides*) is similar to* Solanum crispum *'Autumnale' and to bittersweet or woody nightshade (*Solanum dulcamara*). Any of these may be mistaken for deadly nightshade (*Atropa belladonna*), the most poisonous of the nightshade family.*

closely related to potatoes that it is possible to graft them to give a (poor) crop of both.

The Compositae have many members with daisy-like flowers. One of these is the genus *Senecio*, which has evolved more different species than almost any other genus, yet apart from a few shrubs, border plants and the weeds groundsel and ragwort they are generally unknown and presumably of little use to us. The Compositae include many strong-scented herbs such as *Matricaria* and the artemisias, flowers such as chrysanthemums and Michaelmas daisies and innumerable 'weeds' such as yarrow and tansy. They are frequently good pest repellents.

Umbelliferae are the plants with umbrella-shaped flowerheads. They are common in the flower garden and many root vegetables belong to this family. Carrots have not only been bred to give bigger roots – even the colour has been changed. Carrots used to be purple; the orange colour did not emerge until the early Middle Ages.

The Cruciferae include flowers such as stocks and wallflowers but the most common members of the family are the brassicas. They all have four-petalled, cross-shaped flowers, as have the common and related weeds shepherd's purse and wild radish. Along with most Cruciferae, the brassicas love lime, but the various species have been forced to take many different forms and require very particular conditions if they are to do well. Brussels sprouts, broccoli, kale, cabbage and cauliflowers are all brassicas selected and bred for different uses.

As so many of these near relations are grown in gardens every year, numerous pests and diseases have come to live on them, but they have also been cultivated so long that predators have discovered these pests as a food resource. We can encourage the predators by introducing their companion plants and thus alter the balance in our favour.

PLANTS ASSOCIATED BY ORIGIN

Our desire to grow many plants far from their places of origin means that we have to find or replicate the conditions they would have in their natural habitat as nearly as possible if they are to succeed. This will of course mean introducing other plants typical of that environment. Experience has shown that groups of plants from common origins do better together in the right spot than they do alone. Intelligent gardeners have noted this and follow this policy automatically, whether or not they call it companion planting.

For example, plants from the Mediterranean region are adapted to hotter, drier conditions than they find in northern European climes. The countless different genera we have imported from that region include so many strongly aromatic herbs and silver foliage plants that specialized beds are often made for these plants alone in warm, sheltered, south-facing spots. Mediterranean plants all need the extra warmth and dryness, though each may still have different preferences as to light or heavy soil, lime or acid and so on.

Sometimes plants score a real fluke. *Opuntia* or prickly pear is one of the Cactaceae, yet surprisingly it is just hardy enough to survive British winters in sheltered spots. I have had one unprotected for several years in my silver and grey border. In North America, *Opuntia* species are native and hardy to New England and southern Canada.

Botanical (Latin) names are very useful here because they can help the gardener position a plant correctly. Many of the names refer only to the appearance of a plant or the colour of its flowers, but some tell us which country a species comes from, giving us clues as to its preferences. Fremontodendron *californicum*, Skimmia *japonica*, Cordyline *australis*, Euonymus *europaeus* and Genista *hispanica* are quite easy to locate. Prunus *lusitanica* (Portuguese laurel), Wisteria *sinensis* (Chinese) and Cedrus *atlantica* (from the Atlas mountains of North Africa) are harder to decipher if you don't know Latin. Of course if the area of origin is large, the name does not always tell you what sort of spot the plant will like – the *Fremontodendron* from California is easier to position than the Australian *Cordyline*, as the climate of the latter varies so much more than that of the former.

Specific habitat names are therefore the most useful. Daphne *alpina* comes from the Alps or alpine regions and will probably survive harsher conditions than Clematis *montana* which is only a mountain form. Daphne *rupestris* likes rocks and cliffs and will therefore prefer milder conditions than either. Rosa *arvensis* is so named because it is found in fields and Acer *campestre* on plains and flat ground, while Nicotiana *sylvestris* and Fagus *sylvatica* are very much wild and woodland plants of sylvan glades. (Woodland species often have strong scents, as these are more use than colour in the dark interiors.)

There is no doubting where Gleditsia *aquatica* prefers to be, but Ledum *palustre* is a less easily translatable name for a swamp-loving species. Symphoricarpus *rivularis* is found by rivers and is easy to spot. So too is Crambe *maritima* or sea kale, which grows by the sea, as does Griselinia *littoralis*, but further in shore.

There are confusing names too. Weigela *florida* is floriferous, not from Florida; Leycestria *formosa* is not from Taiwan but from the Himalayas – *formosa* simply means beautiful. Rosa *woodsii* and Rhododendron *forrestii* are not woodland plants; they are named after their discoverers.

Names can be helpful in other ways. Symphytum *officinale* is the right comfrey for herbal uses according to old remedies; the same is true of Salvia *officinalis* and Rosmarinus *officinalis*. Myrtus *communis* and Calluna *vulgaris* are the common or easily found forms. Passiflora *edulis* is edible (but *not* tasty), while Viburnum *utile* is a useful form of a versatile genus (well, at least according to its introducer) and Castanea *sativa* is the cultivated variety of chestnut. Unpleasant scents like those of Iris *foetida* and Hellebore *foetidus* are to be deduced from the names, which may be a handy reminder of their use as pest deterrents. But the disagreeably scented species of rue is Ruta *graveolens*, which is difficult for the non-classicist to decipher.

Names that describe the habit of the plant may also be of use to the companion planter. Juniperus *procumbens* and *Rosmarinus officinalis* 'Prostratus' are low-growing plants you would not want to put at the back of a border. Cotoneaster *horizontalis* is also a spreader and Sarcococca

Wisteria sinensis: the name records its oriental origins; I grow it mostly for its divine scent.

54

humilis is another low-growing species. Watch out for any species called *repens* as these are creeping and rooting plants; *nana* is the name for a dwarf variety. Abies *procera* is a very tall silver fir; Taxus baccata 'Fastigiata' is an erect yew with vertical branches.

Much of the Latin nomenclature is purely descriptive in this way and it would take many pages to explain all the various terms used to describe a plant's leaves, growth or colour. So the species name will only occasionally be of help. However, knowing any plant's genus should at least give you an idea of what general conditions it will prefer.

Most gardeners divide their garden up in established ways that already take account of these associations. As mentioned above, the plants we put in the herbaceous border have been preselected from many, largely because they are adapted to most common soils and conditions. Silver- and grey-foliaged borders contain so many plants from the Mediterranean and other more arid climates that they are only suited to hot, dry, sheltered spots. The tenderer plants from still warmer climes are confined to the cool greenhouse, conservatory or hothouse depending on how much heat they require. Many enthusiasts group alpine plants together and grow them because they are so compact and take little space, but also because they need similar conditions which are not easy to provide. In a mixed flowerbed they would be lost and rapidly overwhelmed; rock gardens and screes provide them with approximations to their original conditions but require a lot of weeding to keep out more vigorous neighbours. The most exacting need alpine houses as they detest the damp air of lower altitudes, being adapted to the much colder but drier mountain air.

Shrub borders are full of plants that are by nature the creators of woodland conditions and thus they rapidly produce the habitat they like. But do not forget the individual needs of each plant: some may prefer more open, glade-like conditions, despite the advantages of shelter. Roses

This narrow shrub border relies on foliage interest with a magnolia top left, golden elder (Sambucus nigra 'Aurea') left, a variegated holly centre and the more floriferous laurel 'Otto Luycken' on the right.

in particular fare badly when choked by other shrubs which make them more prone to disease.

Different shrubs from the same habitat are easily combined, but start mixing them and some will suffer. Ericaceae, the heathers, will obviously thrive together in acid soil, but these soils will be hostile to plants that like lime and vice versa. Put a mountain dwarf in amongst hedgerow natives and it will be choked in a matter of weeks.

All the common soft fruits are woodland-edge plants and have similar requirements, which is fortunate as they have to be squeezed together into a fruit cage (see p. 126). Woodland plants have adapted to light shade and humus-rich soils, so they dislike being on hot, dry walls with poor, thin soil. Cliff- and rock-climbers like grapevines revel in these conditions and of course the extra warmth is suitable for more tender plants like *Trachelospermum*, jasmine or passionflowers. However, if the wall faces north or is lightly shaded with some moisture at the base, it will then be more suited to roses and the like.

The white lace-capped hydrangeas are tougher plants, more adapted to woodland settings and poor soils than the more colourful blue and pink flowering forms.

Plants change according to conditions and other plants

Most of the plants we grow are closely related, having developed from one primitive ancestor to the vast number of forms we know today. Different paths of evolution enabled plants to adapt themselves to conditions prevailing in most parts of the planet. They discovered various ways of coping with each situation, with the result that almost all environmental niches support several different species. These may come from families which are only distantly related but resemble each other closely as they use the same strategies for survival. For instance, hot, dry conditions cause water losses, so many plants have evolved ways of combating this. A common solution is stopping the water vapour escaping by trapping it in a shroud of fine hairs, thorns or powdery farina which then causes a silvery appearance. *Helichrysum angustifolium* and other *Helichrysum* species, *Rosmarinus officinalis* 'Prostratus', *Salvia tricolor* and most species of *Veronica* are examples of plants that have adapted in this way. The adaptation then tends to make them prone to damage from damp and they often require special care in moister climes.

In unfettered nature, plants are chosen to associate with others through the process of succession – only those plants which are most suited to any given conditions are 'selected' by the environment. Those that in growth are intolerant of dry conditions are unlikely to germinate in them at all. Boggy conditions will rot the seeds of plants that prefer dry spots. Plants that need strong sun will wither away soon after germination if they come up in shade from trees or dense weeds. For example, if mixed seed of the bedstraws is sown, the heath form (*Galium saxatile*) will only survive in non-calcerous soil, while the mountain form (*G. asperum*) will predominate if chalk is added. In the UK, a heavy clay soil will almost invariably have hoary plantains, stinking mayweed and brown bent growing in it, a light acid soil mercuries, daisies and small nettles.

These selection processes carry on continuously, so that the self-sown plants growing in a place not only indicate the conditions but themselves modify those conditions. As seedlings in bare soil the first ones to emerge have the advantage of first bite of any nutrients and as soon as they are established they try to shade out any plants following them or to combat them with root and leaf secretions and gases like ethylene. If there is a shortage of any nutrient, the plant that succeeds will be the one that is most efficient at grabbing it. As we have seen, weeds are excellent accumulators of nutrients in short supply and this is a major reason why they need controlling. However, it also means they are the best plants for restoring depleted nutrients, as each succeeding generation leaves rotting root hairs, detritus and leaf litter. They extract more completely nutrients they specifically need and change the make-up of the soil until they are themselves no longer well suited to it.

These Iceland poppies (Papaver nudicaule) *are colonizing this gravel as it resembles their native habitat; the shrubby mallow also likes the conditions in this corner, although it is a native from nearly 1600 km (1000 miles) further south: it benefits from the heat the gravel throws up.*

As the conditions created by the plants first colonizing an area are eventually changed by those very plants and become unsuitable for them, others replace them, and so it goes on until a maintainable balance is achieved. In many climates long-term stability would be reached with forests, but where grazing animals are introduced grasslands predominate, as grasses are able to grow despite grazing. Most plants grow from the tip, but grasses grow from the base, so cutting off the leaf deprives the plant of productive leaf area and the resources it took to make it, but does not arrest its growth. Plants that extend from the tip are destroyed by grazing unless they can throw a new growth from a bud lower down. In addition to grasses, grazing therefore selects for plants that either produce plentiful buds, spread rapidly with runners close to the ground or have low, tight rosettes that animals cannot nibble. Rosette plants only survive in newly exposed ground or where grazing keeps down competitors, as they are rapidly choked by taller-growing plants.

Other plants that succeed despite grazing are those that are prickly, thorny or distasteful. Unfortunately, these modifications do not protect them from a new grazing peril, the lawnmower. This mimics a grazing animal and arrests natural succession, but you only have to leave a lawn unmown for a few months to see how quickly nature takes over again. Fine lawn becomes meadow, then rough grass with herbaceous weeds forming great clumps, and within a year shrubby plants will be establishing themselves. In three years it will probably be woodland edge with tree seedlings above head height and flourishing bramble patches.

Carefully maintained lawns can thus be regarded as overgrazed meadows and an arrested succession, so we need to modify treatment accordingly. The strong-growing grasses will outcompete mosses, resist wear and stand poorer conditions than 'bowling green' ones. The latter may produce a fine sward but they grow poorly and are subject to many failings. To increase the quantity and value of 'hay' or clippings, the tougher grasses are best not grown alone but with clovers and herbs added. Lawns are then greener, and they smell and look wonderful.

So the companion gardener tries to move with nature and not fight her. Introducing clover doesn't mean putting in a weed that competes; it is adding a friend that feeds the grass, keeping it greener longer in times of drought. Admittedly some otherwise useful plants like thistles have unpleasant characteristics and need eradicating. Any plant that is detrimental to the others or displeasing to us can fairly be regarded as a weed that needs controlling. This can be done by altering the conditions in favour of the preferred plants and to the detriment of the weeds. When creeping buttercup starts to increase it is likely to indicate that the soil is becoming more acid – a dressing of calcified seaweed or lime will correct this and the buttercup infestation will decrease, though it is unlikely to disappear completely until a couple of years of treatment have passed.

Other conditions that can be changed include fertility, nutrient balance, texture or aeration. This will affect the mix of plants but in terms of proportion rather than of species. In other words, you are likely to have the same plants but in different numbers – conditions have to change radically for new species to appear.

Grass and lawns are the ideal foil for flowers and the interplay of light and shade.

What is true for the lawn is also true for other areas of the garden. Certain species of plants are going to do well in any given place and will predominate over all the others. Trees and climbers will always tend to exclude most other woody plants, but unless they cast very heavy or evergreen shade there is usually a layer of carpet plants underneath. These carpet plants utilize the topmost layer of soil, so are not outcompeted by the deeper roots of the trees, and they are frequently adapted to grabbing winter light when the trees are out of leaf.

Geranium ibericum *and* G. sanguineum *are among the best groundcover carpeting plants, thriving in partial shade.*

No matter how well you look after them, plants put into unsuitable places cannot do as well as those that are better adapted, especially if the latter are already there. If a plant is suited to its conditions, it will be very good at preventing any other plant getting started. The only way to succeed with a new planting in an established garden is to use plants even more suited to the conditions. Thus your choice is more limited than if you are planning a new area. In either case the microclimate and conditions require you to put in suitable plants and adjust the balance in favour of one or other with spacing, feeding and position. If you don't make the right choices initially, you may lose your plants or face continual corrective treatment for poor growth, pests and diseases.

The plants that will be most suited to a given place will probably belong to several whole genera rather than to individual species. Because evolution has produced more and more specialization we find that, although families of plants are spread over many areas, each family member or genus is usually particularly suited to some general conditions and the individual species within the genus are more specifically adapted to variations within those conditions.

As such factors as soil content or availability of water change, plants either adapt or are outcompeted. Some plants have different forms as possibilities within a general plan to help them deal with a wider range of conditions. In different circumstances the same seed may produce different ratios of male and female seedlings, for example, or taller or shorter plants with larger or fewer flower heads. This mutability helps any species adapt to minor variations, but even so, if you put them in the wrong place, there will always be other plants better equipped to cope.

Plants respond to minute changes. The differences between one spot and another may not be readily apparent, but the plants will still react to them. Providing competition is kept down, many garden plants flourish in a wide number of situations. Stop weeding and pruning, and succession returns; the plants in the right places hold their own, but all the rest will be overwhelmed in a season or two. Because of this it is always educational to look at derelict gardens. It is not just the toughest that endure – all the survivors are giving a clear indication of their preferences.

Microclimates and soils vary so much from spot to spot that the plant distribution in a small patch can be every bit as diverse as across much larger areas. A hedge beside a ditch is not one habitat or set of conditions but many, depending on variables such as scale, aspect and type of hedge. Each variation will affect plants and change the species over time.

PLANTS ASSOCIATED BY THEIR NATURE AND FORM

Plants have adapted in many different ways, producing forms that are long- and short-lived, that grow quickly and seed or spread with roots. Some have tough growth that lasts, others have woody stems that get bigger over the years, still others may appear and disappear in a single season. The way any plant grows affects how we accommodate it and it is often best grouped with others of the same habit. Once we have categorized our plants, it is easier to plan their futures.

Hollyhocks (Althaea rosea) *are best grown as biennials.*

Annuals, biennials, perennials

Annuals die within a year (though cool season hardy annuals may survive the winter), biennials are grown to die after flowering, while perennials would flower for ever, if the plants survived.

Most annuals grown for flowers do well in poor soil as this encourages flowering; over-rich conditions promote lush growth and fewer flowers. But those rich, moist conditions are necessary for the annuals we grow for food, such as lettuce and spinach, otherwise the leaves do poorly. Those grown for seed like peas and beans fall in between, but have the advantage of making their own fertility once they are established.

Biennials grow in the first year and store energy so that they can make seed the next year, but we may eat the storage organ before then. Sometimes they try to flower in the first year; this is called bolting and is mostly caused by checks to growth. Carrots, onions, leeks, beetroot and most of the brassicas are biennial but are almost always eaten before we see their flowers.

In the ornamental garden some plants which tend to become scruffy after two seasons are treated as biennials, even though left to themselves they would be short-lived perennials: wallflowers, foxgloves and hollyhocks are examples.

Foxgloves are treated as biennials, so they must be planted two years in succession and allowed to self-seed if you want flowers every year: you will soon find you have lots.

Perennials do not live for ever, but some may be very long-lived; most plants in a garden are gone in a few decades, though some trees may last for hundreds of years. In the vegetable garden asparagus may be productive for twenty or thirty years while strawberries are effectively perennial, but in practical terms need replacing every third or fourth year. Blackcurrants and raspberries are similar – they would live longer than ten years or so, but rarely do well after that length of time because of the build-up of virus diseases.

In the flower garden, plants are continually being replaced naturally with new ones, but the process goes unnoticed: many of the bulbous plants produce a new bulb or corm every year, leaving the old one to wither away. Some make the new bulb above the old and this accounts for the annoying way they seem to push themselves out of the ground. The same happens with garlic, where each clove pushes itself out sideways atop its roots. Leeks produce bulbils if they are deflowered, as the reproductive energy is diverted from seed production. With plants that are allowed to set seed the converse happens: further growth is reduced, as the energy is directed to seed production. Hence the need to dead-head roses and other flowering plants and to nip out bolting shallots. One plant flowering may cause others of the same species to do likewise, so a bolter must be removed before it causes others to bolt.

Shrubs, trees or herbaceous plants

Trees can be defined as bigger shrubs with a single stem, but the attribute unique to trees and shrubs is that they have woody parts which survive above ground all year. Shrubs can be mixed with other plants, but will usually choke them if not pruned back regularly. Even when kept to themselves in a shrub border the strongest growers will tend to predominate unless you keep them in check.

Herbaceous plants may leave some withered growth above ground, but generally regrow from the roots each year. Semi-shrubby plants like fuchsias may have herbaceous habits when the winters are cold enough to kill the shrubby growth but mild enough to spare the roots. Buddleias and some other shrubs can be made to appear to have the herbaceous habit by pruning away the top growth annually.

Many herbaceous plants are extremely vigorous: of these, those that spread sideways need splitting up and replanting every few years to stop them taking over. Then the plant becomes to all intents and purposes immortal – some of our garden flowers may well be bits of plants originally subdivided in Roman times.

The need for splitting and replanting together with the dismal appearance of most of these plants in winter has led us to group them together in the uniquely English herbaceous border. Plants have been selected for this purpose over decades and thus those commonly grown are remarkably tolerant of variations in soil and other conditions. A few plants that are not really herbaceous at all are included for our convenience and pleasure – shrubs pruned herbaceously, for example, and some bulbs and small soft shrubs like pinks (*Dianthus*) and rock rose (*Helianthemum*).

Most of the plants in the foreground will disappear completely during the winter, while the framework of shrubby plants will endure. Note the delicate pink-flowered Dicentra spectabilis *in the centre by the pool: it must have a rich, moist position like this if it is to thrive.*

64

Hardy or tender plants

Obviously plants commonly found outdoors in the UK are hardy and can endure our winters unprotected. Many plants are not quite hardy and may survive a few years before being killed in a hard season. Often it is the damp period following the cold that does the most harm and then it is more important to keep plants dry than to keep them warm. Rosemary used to be considered too delicate to be grown out of doors in the UK, but it is now very popular – it may have adapted slowly to colder conditions. Pelargoniums rarely survive British winters unaided, fuchsias come again from the roots while *Lippia citriodora*, the real lemon verbena, soon expires if it is not looked after. All these plants can be protected with groundcover or dry straw where winters are very mild, in the US zones 8 and south.

Plants started from seed fall into three categories depending on their cold tolerance. Tender annuals need the most warmth at all stages, including germination. They should not be planted out until the weather has settled and become reliably warm. In cool climates like the UK, they may do best when kept under cover for the entire growing season. Half-hardy annuals tolerate little or no frost, but will grow well if protected early in the season. The seedlings of hardy annuals are reasonably frost tolerant. They often germinate in the open ground in early spring while it is still quite cold.

Short- and long-season plants vary in the number of days of growth needed from germination to successful cropping. This is why so many plants such as tomatoes and sweet corn are started off under cover. If they were sown direct in the open ground in the UK they would not have long enough to produce crops before the autumn frosts killed them. We could protect them at that end of the season, but it is easier to do so in the spring when they are still small and while the days get longer, with more sunlight.

In a similar manner early and main-crop varieties are shorter and longer season versions of the same species. Pink Duke of York is a very early potato, but it is no more or less hardy than King Edward, which is main crop. If you plant them together around Eastertime, the early will have produced edible new potatoes by the end of May and died about the end of July, giving a modest harvest. The main crop will not give any edible tubers till July but will carry on growing into September, finally yielding more weight.

PLANTS SUITED TO CERTAIN CONDITIONS

There are so many different plants in cultivation that whole books list their requirements. But most of the common ones are grown because they are tolerant of most conditions in average soils. In general plants need soil that is never dry or waterlogged, has some lime or is only slightly acid, and is in sun or light shade. However, there are many exceptions – plants that are useful or attractive, but which are more demanding than the average and will not thrive without certain conditions. Some species have adapted to acid soils that contain no lime, or to semi-desert conditions, or to light

Be a good companion: give your plants their favourite conditions and they will reward you. Here are a couple of the dozen melons grown in a cold frame in the warm moisture atop a big compost heap.

shade. Their requirements may change as other conditions change: for example, many plants such as *Skimmia* do not like lime, but tolerate it more when they are grown in moist, light shade. Some have strong preferences and these are noted in the boxes. As mentioned before, individual species tend to conform to the characteristics of the genus
.

Wet or dry

Plants that like wet spots may not survive actual waterlogging or submersion for long periods and if the soil is wet because of clay it will probably be acid as well. Wet acid soil can be limed to make it suitable for plants that need it, but it is impractical to try the converse and remove lime. Vegetables generally need moist, not wet, soil, though celery and celeriac will thrive in damper conditions. Runner beans, peas, carrots and overwintered crops will do especially badly if waterlogged. Planting willows, poplars and alders helps dry out the soil but they will compete with your crops. The dogwoods (*Cornus*) do well in the wet, but like most shrubs they rarely survive if they are immersed for long.

Herbaceous plants do better, monsters like *Gunnera manicata* give a tropical swamp effect in a wet area. See the box opposite for a list of herbaceous plants that thrive in damp conditions. One of the most important plants for wet areas is comfrey, which will extract nutrients and provide an excellent source of fertility.

Azaleas and rhododendrons can give fantastic colours but need lime-free soil.

ACID OR LIME

Plants that do not like lime are called calcifuges; the following genera all need lime-free soil:
Andromeda, Arctostaphylos, Azalea, Calluna, Camellia, Cassiope, Clethra, Cryptomeria, many *Erica, Fothergilla, Gaultheria, Gentiana, Hamamelis*, some *Hydrangea* (depending on type and the colour of flower desired), *Itea, Kalmia, Larix*, many lilies, *Leucothoe*, most *Magnolia, Myrica, Pernettya, Pieris, Pinus*, some *Primula, Rhododendron, Sarcococca, Skimmia, Staphylea, Stewartia, Vaccinium.*

In the productive garden, strawberries and raspberries prefer soil to be more acid than lime; the bog plants like blueberry and cranberry need very wet, acid conditions and prefer no lime.

Plants that will grow in limey soil are legion, as most either need or tolerate lime. If you have problems with chalky soils, it is most likely to be because the soil is a thin layer, short of organic material and thus hot and dry. Some plants such as the brooms and brassicas seem to revel in lime, and the following also thrive:
Acer, Aesculus, Alnus, Amelanchier, Berberis, Betula, Buddleia, Ceanothus, Cerasus, Chaenomeles, Cistus, Clematis, Cornus, Corylus, Cotoneaster, Crataegus, Cytisus, Deutzia, Elaeagnus, Escallonia, Euonymus, Fagus, Fraxinus, Garrya, Gypsophila, Hypericum, Ilex, Jasminum, Kerria, Lavandula, Leycesteria, Ligustrum, Linum, Lupinus, Philadelphus, Populus, Pyrus, Quercus, Rhus, Ribes, Rosa, Salix, Scabiosa, Spartium, Spiraea, Tamarix, Tilia, Ulnus, Viburnum.

Most plants will show chlorosis and other signs of progressive mineral deficiency in very alkaline (lime) soil. This can be corrected for all except the calcifuges by adding moisture and plenty of organic material.

Primulas and ferns revel in damp places, as do: *Acorus, Arum, Aruncus, Astilbe, Caltha, Clethra, Cimcifuge, Dodecatheon, Eriophorum, Filipendula, Glyceria, Hemerocallis* (which also do well in the dry), *Hosta,* some *Iris* (another group of this genus also does well in the dry), *Ligularia, Mimulus, Myrica, Ranunculus aquatilus, Rodgersia, Spiraea, Trollius.*

*Comfrey (*Symphytum *spp.) and teasels (*Dipsacus fullonum*) are excellent companions from the wild garden for this damp area around my pond. Both give good groundcover and nectar for beneficial birds and insects. The comfrey is cut to the ground after flowering and turned into a rich liquid feed for other plants in the garden.*

*The day-lilies (*Hemerocallis*) thrive almost anywhere, hot and dry or cool and moist. This variety is 'Corky'.*

   Plants that do well in hot, dry spots need care and watering to help them become established before they can be left to look after themselves. Nearly hardy plants can survive many winters in such a place; cacti such as *Opuntia* and bulbs such as nerines, *Amaryllis* and *Crinum* thrive at the base of a warm wall in cool climates. The Mediterranean and silver-leaved plants like hot, dry conditions as do most herbs, but not vegetables unless they are watered thoroughly. If you establish them well grapes and figs will really burgeon and send roots to depths where water can be found. Apricots, peaches and nectarines may also thrive if the soil is rich and well mulched. See box opposite for recommended species for hot, dry areas.

Sun or shade

All plants need sunlight, especially the Mediterranean herbs, but some prefer to have it only part of the time or to be in light shade all day. Apart from ferns and mosses, hardly any plants grow in intense shade, and then only if they are kept moist as well. Many trees and climbers are adapted to shade as seedlings and will grow towards the light and block it, so if you grow them in shaded places they will soon make them shadier.

Dry shade is the most difficult situation: few plants tolerate it, though various plants have adapted to some degree (see box overleaf).

Light shade suits many plants, especially those like Solomon's seal (Polygonatum multiflorum) *which come originally from a woodland habitat.*

Sun-loving plants such as the cotton lavender (Santolina) *and English lavender* (Lavandula) *edging this path can cope with a little light shade if they are dry, but rot rapidly in damp shade. If the shade becomes too heavy they soon become drawn and thin.*

Sedums and wild strawberries make good groundcover for hot, dry spots.

PLANTS FOR HOT AND DRY AREAS

The following genera are mostly adapted to dry conditions and provide some tough plants:
Achillea, Alyssum, Artemisia, Aubretia, Berberis, Buddleia, Ceanothus, Cheiranthus, Cineraria, Cistus, Cosmos, Cytisus, Dianthus, Euphorbia, Eryngium, Eschscholzia, Foeniculum, Iris, Genista, Hebe, Helianthemum, Hemerocallis, many *Iris, Lavandula, Linum, Malva, Matricaria, Montbretia, Nepeta, Papaver, Passiflora, Pelargonium, Robinia, Rosmarinus, Spartium, Solanum, Salvia, Sedum, Sempervivum, Stachys, Tanacetum, Taxus, Thymus, Yucca.*

Little grows in heavy, dry shade, but add moisture and you can often grow comfrey, mints, nettles and possibly violets in heavy shade, as well as the ferns and mosses mentioned above. In less heavy shade and rich, moist soil many plants will succeed, including some fruits and vegetables. Rhubarb will grow almost anywhere and all the currants and berries are woodland plants adapted to light shade. Chives, horseradish and parsley will tolerate shade; beetroot, cabbage, lettuce, radish and spinach grow but tend to be poor or lank if the light is really too low. Some other vegetables will succeed if sown or even better planted out late to catch the brighter summer months or if the shade is only for part of the day, but they would perform better in full sun: this applies to broad beans, carrots, Chinese cabbage, courgettes (zucchini), kale, kohlrabi, leeks, parsnips, peas, potatoes and most leafy saladings.

Many of the ornamental plants listed for wet places (see box p. 68) do not mind light shade, and some prefer it. Variegated and yellow-leaved versions may burn in full sun, while some lose their colouring if the shade is too heavy. Always prune out any growths that have reverted to plain coloration on variegated plants. See box for plants that will endure darker, moister shade than most.

PLANTS WHICH TOLERATE DRY SHADE

Acer, Ajuga, Alchemilla, Aucuba, Berberis, Bergenia, Betula, Brunnera, Buxus, Cortaderia, Cotoneaster, Crataegus, Epimedium, Euonymus, Geranium and the tender related *Pelargonium, Hedera, Ilex, Iris* (yet again – this tribe is very adaptable and moves into every niche), *Lamium, Lonicera, Mahonia, Osmanthus, Pachysandra, Pittosporum, Prunus laurocerasus, Pulmonaria, Populus, Rhus, Ribes, Robinia, Rubus, Ruscus, Sambucus, Skimmia, Santolina, Sorbus, Symphoricarpos, Vinca, Waldsteinia.*

PLANTS FOR DARK, MOIST SHADE

Plants that will tolerate these conditions are found mostly among the following genera: *Alchemilla, Aruncus, Astilbe, Aucuba, Azalea, Caltha, Camellia, Cornus, Daphne, Elaeagnus, Fatsia, Fragaria, Hedera, Helleborus, Hemerocallis, Hosta, Hydrangea, Ligularia, Ligustrum, Lythrum, Monarda, Mentha, Osmanthus, Pachysandra, Pernettya, Pieris, Polygonatum, Polygonum, Rheum, Rhododendron, Rubus, Ruscus, Salix, Sambucus, Sarcococca, Skimmia, Spiraea, Symphoricarpos, Vinca.*

Golden feverfew (Chrysanthemum parthenium *'Aureum') and Rose of Sharon (*Hypericum calycinum) *may be useful groundcover plants for almost anywhere in the garden – but they will not be content to stay in any confined space!*

Irises are tough plants rarely bothered by conditions that would inhibit many others. They cope and thrive in many different and difficult spots. The yellow and purple irises top left set each other off strikingly, while purple irises also make an eye-catching border with the strong red of the tulips, above.

Above: *Cowslips and Good King Henry* (Chenopodium bonus-Henricus) *flourish in the moist conditions near a garden pond.*

Left: *Primroses love rich, moist soil and thrive in light shade. Stachys lanata, with its grey, felted leaves, is a stranger to such a position and will never prosper.*

The Renegades – Weeds and What They Indicate

One useful feature of weeds is that they tell you about the conditions they are growing in: the plants best suited to any given condition are those most likely to be found where that condition applies. One type of weed may occur by chance; the presence of several that all like the same conditions is very likely to be indicative of those conditions. Left to itself for any length of time, an area would support only the natural 'weeds', the trees, shrubs and other plants most suited to it. As already discussed, this fact will over a period change the conditions and thus the prevailing vegetation. The box on the right lists 'weeds' that are likely to occur on certain soil types.

On prospective land you want to see masses of stinging nettles! Other favourable weeds are chickweed, forget-me-not, goosegrass, groundsel, thistles and yarrow. All these indicate a rich, fertile soil suitable for most purposes. What you most definitely do not want, and it may be best to move home if they are already there, are white-flowered bindweed, equisetum, horseradish, Japanese knotweed, lesser celandine (*Ficaria verna*), Leyland cypress hedges or poplars on or near the sunny side, oxalis and winter heliotrope. Some generally feared weeds are common, very tough and require several attacks a week apart before they die, but they do succumb to persistence; these include brambles, coltsfoot, couch grass, creeping buttercup, docks, ground elder, knotweed, any nettles, thistles, tree saplings. The box lists some other plants that may become weeds if allowed to establish themselves.

'WEEDS' OR NATIVE PLANTS THAT OCCUR MOST FREQUENTLY ON ACID SOIL

Betony, birch, black bindweed, broom, cinquefoil, corn chamomile, cornflower, corn marigold, corn spurrey, daisy, foxglove, fumitory, gorse, harebell, heather, horse or marestail, lesser periwinkle, mercury, pansy, rhododendron, rowan, scabious, shepherd's cress, small nettle, Scots pine, sorrel, spurrey, tormentil.

'WEEDS OR NATIVE PLANTS THAT OCCUR MOST FREQUENTLY ON LIME SOIL

Agrimony, bellflower, black medick, candytuft, cat's ear, *Clematis*, cornelian cherry, cowslip, dogwood, goat's beard, greater hawkbit, hawthorn, hazel, horseshoe vetch, knapweed, lamb's lettuce, mignonette, ox-eye daisy, penny cress, privet, rosebriar, salad burnet, spindle, stonecrop, tansy, valerian, wallflower, white mustard, wild carrot, yarrow.

'WEEDS' OR NATIVE PLANTS THAT OCCUR MOST FREQUENTLY IN HEAVY CLAY

Annual meadow grass, creeping buttercup, cowslip, goosegrass, hoary and ribwort plantain, meadow cranesbill, nipplewort, selfheal, silverweed.

GARDEN PLANTS THAT CAN RAPIDLY BECOME WEEDS

The following are common plants that should be treated firmly as they easily get out of hand: where a generic name is given, this applies to most or all species of the genus. *Allium, Ajuga, Alstroemeria,* bellflowers, English bluebells (*Endymion*), brambles, *Brunnera,* lesser celandine (*Ficaria verna*), euphorbias, feverfew, forget-me-nots, foxgloves, goldenrod, grape hyacinth, grapevines, Himalayan balsam, honesty, *Hypericum, Iris foetidissima, Lamium,* Leyland cypress hedges, loosestrife (*Lysimachia, Lythrum*), mints, *Nepeta, Oxalis, Polemonium, Polygonum,* poplars, pot marigolds (*Calendula*), poppies, privet, Russian creeper (*Polygonum baldschuanicum*), *Pulmonaria,* Shasta daisies, Sedum, sweet rocket, *Sisyrinchium,* sycamore (*Acer pseudoplatanus*), *Vinca, Viola,* willows.

Above: *The loosestrifes* Lysimachia ciliata *and* Lythrum salicaria *are both good plants for attracting bees and useful 'fillers' in damp areas, but may spread out of control.*

Below: *Sisyrinchiums are survivors and can grow most anywhere and everywhere.*

'WEEDS' OR NATIVE PLANTS THAT OCCUR MOST FREQUENTLY ON LIGHT, DRY SOIL

Annual nettle, bramble, broad dock, bulbous buttercup, charlock, dandelion, groundsel, knotgrass, mouse-eared chickweed, stinging nettle, petty spurge, poppy, red deadnettle, rosebay willow herb, shepherd's purse, speedwell.

'WEEDS' OR NATIVE PLANTS THAT OCCUR MOST FREQUENTLY IN WETTER PLACES

Alder, bugle, bulrush, buttercup, comfrey, cuckoo flower, dock, great willow herb, hemp agrimony, Himalayan balsam, loosestrife, marsh marigold, meadowsweet, mint, plantain, primrose, ragged robin, sedge, stinging nettle, thistle, water avens, willow.

SOME USEFUL WEEDS

By no means all 'weeds' are pernicious: here are a number that are worth encouraging for a variety of reasons:

Dandelion *Taraxacum officinale*
An edible weed, it accumulates calcium and silica. It increases humus and is deep rooting but gives off ethylene gas, inhibiting the growth of nearby plants and causing plants and fruit to ripen prematurely. Grows well in the same conditions as alfalfa and eventually supplants it. It deters Colorado beetles and is a host to predatory wasps. Protects tomatoes from *Fusarium* wilt.

Dead nettle *Lamium album*
A nectar producer over a long season, this thrives in damp shady spots. It is generally beneficial to vegetables and should be encouraged. The red form is as valuable as the white and is prettier. Plants of either may help deter potato bugs.

Fat hen *Chenopodium album*
A common weed that used to be eaten like asparagus, as did its cousin Good King Henry. It is very rich in calcium and high in Vitamins A and C. It aids other plants if it is not allowed to overwhelm them, particularly sweet corn and potatoes. With the latter it seeds before it can be seen to be weeded. It is of benefit to the cucurbits and many flowers. It can be used as a sacrificial plant, attracting leaf miners, and may also help keep pigs free of roundworm.

Stinging nettle *Urtica dioica*
Needs little description to Europeans, but the beneficial effects on plants growing around nettles are manifold. Nettles cause herbs to give more and stronger aromatic oils, they aid composting and help fruit to ripen, yet stop it going mouldy. Nettle tea is used for its stimulating effect and fungicidal properties. As a liquid feed it is excellent combined with comfrey. Dried nettles are good for all livestock, cooked they are good for us. The remedy for stings of rubbing in dock juice is nearly always to hand as the plants usually occur together. If a patch is cleared the soil is usually a wonderful dark humus, rich in iron. Scavenge your surroundings for nettles to add to the compost, but leave some in the sun for caterpillars to feed on.

Thistle
Small amounts of sowthistle (*Sonchus*) may aid tomatoes, onions, the cucurbits and sweet corn. True thistles (*Cirsium*) are unwanted companions in most lawns, but easily hand weeded. They accumulate potassium and are deep rooting, so really should be encouraged. However, the prickles are horrible, so either hoe them out weekly or wait till they are flowering and pull them then. They suppress oats and harbour mangold fly and bean aphids. Canadian thistle (*Cirsium arvense*) accumulates iron, but is outlawed in many parts of the US because of its rampantly invasive nature.

Foxgloves, lovely as they are, can rapidly become weeds.

THE OTHER COMPANIONS: WILDLIFE ENCOURAGEMENT LARGE AND SMALL

The greater part of good gardening method lies in encouraging all the forms of life in the soil and above the ground. If there is little life in the soil, there will be fewer larger forms of wildlife in the garden. The more wildlife big or small in the garden, the more plant life it can support, and this in turn promotes more life and more plants.

Soil life may be encouraged and nurtured with watering, mulches, compost, planting the best companions and avoiding soluble fertilizers and pesticides. Why stay where there is nothing to eat? The multitude of insect and scurrying life is increased by growing many diverse plants providing food, water, shelter, nesting and wintering sites. Larger forms of life are thus enticed to these and can be encouraged with yet more plants. However, a well-planned companion garden is not just filled with all the plants that benefit wildlife; every nook and cranny is packed with nest boxes for birds of all sizes, bat roosts, hedgehog dens, frog and toad pits, ladybird nests and piles of rotten logs in shady corners.

More pests can survive in the average garden than would be present in the wild because of the diversity of food sources. These in turn support larger populations of predators and parasites which keep them in check. The natural balance this reaches is not necessarily the one that suits us and we try to move it in our favour by aiding the beneficial insects.

Increasing and spreading the flowering season throughout more of the year will encourage insects, especially bees. It is ironic that nowadays city beekeepers do better than their country cousins. The growth of cities has impoverished country wildlife with the incessant taking over of land for building, roads and food production. There are now so few areas of uncultivated land and wild flowers that many country beekeepers despair while city gardens are filling with expensively planted flowers. Beekeepers who live in cities also find that the shelter and warmth from all the buildings extends the honey season by many weeks.

Even if we do not keep bees, each of us can put a few bee plants in somewhere and it is really in our interest to do so. In the short term we benefit from pollination of our fruits and flowers, and more honey, but in the long term we may save ourselves. If bees die out whole families of plants will disappear and the chain of ecological damage may take us with it. Bumble bees are even more valuable than honey bees, although of course they give no honey. They are useful early in the year because they fly in colder conditions and pollinate the early flowers. Both honey bees and bumble bees need continuous supplies of pollen and nectar, so grow as many different flowers as you can to spread the season.

A third group of bees, the leaf-cutters, pollinate early fruit; they benefit from the same plants as the others (see box on p. 77).

Butterflies are not pest controllers and may themselves be pests in disguise. However they may pollinate and their beauty is reason enough to encourage them. Most flowers can feed them as they have long tongues (though of course many rely on specific plants for the caterpillar stage). See box on p. 78 for a list of plants to encourage butterflies.

Seats attract people and encourage them to pause and appreciate the scene.

Hoverflies are the best aphid eaters we can encourage; the larvae eat many more in a day than ladybird larvae. See box on page 79 for a list of plants hoverflies like.

Ladybirds, lacewings and predatory wasps may take nectar from the same plants as hoverflies, but the best encouragement is plenty of food. Grow plants that are regularly laden with aphids and there will soon be predators.

Wasps are very good friends in the spring and summer when they eat pests, but become pests when autumn comes as they eat all the fruit! All the nectar producers for hoverflies will aid these and their relatives, the predatory wasps which parasitize caterpillars, beetles, aphids and spiders. Dead rotting wood will provide wasps with the raw material for their nests.

BEE PLANTS

Most of all honey bees go for bluish or whitish flowers, but other colours are not excluded. The following garden flower genera commonly grown in beds and borders have built up a close relationship with bees and will attract them: *Aconitum, Allium, Anchusa, Arabis, Aster, Borago, Campanula, Centaurea, Chionodoxa, Colchicum, Delphinium, Echinops, Echium, Endymion, Erigeron, Hyssopus, Lavandulus, Limnanthes, Limonium, Lobelia, Lychnis, Lysimachia, Lythrum, Malva, Matricaria, Melissa, Mentha, Monarda, Muscari, Myositis, Nemophila, Nepeta, Nigella, Omphalodes, Origanum, Papaver, Phacelia, Platycodon, Polemonium, Pulmonaria, Reseda, Salvia, Scabiosa, Scilla, Thymus, Veronica.*

Trees and shrubs have also come to depend on bees and limes or lindens are well known for filling hives with honey. Most members of the following genera are good for bees, but avoid sterile double-flowered varieties: *Acer, Aesculus, Alnus, Berberis, Betula, Caragana, Catalpa, Ceanothus, Cercis, Chaenomeles, Cistus, Cotoneaster, Crataegus, Daphne, Elaeagnus, Escallonia, Fagus, Fraxinus, Fuchsia, Hedera, Hypericum, Ilex, Laurus, Liquidambar, Liriodendron, Malus, Mespilus, Olearia, Perovskia, Physiocarpus, Populus, Potentilla, Prunus, Pyracantha, Quercus, Rhamnus, Rhus, Ribes, Robinia, Rosmarinus, Rubus, Salix, Salvia, Senecio, Skimmia, Sorbus, Spiraea, Symphoricarpos, Syringa, Tamarix, Tilia, Ulex, Viburnum, Weigela.*

In the vegetable and fruit garden, leave unwanted brassicas, leeks and onions to go to flower, as bees love these. Strawberries, especially the alpine ones, are always popular but raspberries, blackberries and their hybrids are even better. Clovers sown in sward and as groundcover or green manure are one of the biggest attractants; on farms field bean and oilseed rape are the bees' favourites. Sweet basil, summer savory, lemon balm and the mints are all much loved. The mints are probably the most cost-effective for large areas as they spread so well.

Weeds are, of course, by definition, unwanted but the flowers of these are loved by bees: Agrimony, bellflower, betony, corncockle, clovers, cranesbill, flax, forget-me-not, hound's tongue, mallow, meadowsweet, melilot, mullin, ox-eye daisy, pansy, poppy, ragged robin, scabious, soapwort, tansy, teasel, trefoil, valerian, viper's bugloss, yarrow.

Bumble bees prefer the following: *Aubretia, Berberis*, English bluebells (*Endymion*), dandelions, flowering currants, wallflowers and white deadnettle, which are most needed in early spring. From early summer they go for brambles and their hybrids, buddleias, clovers, comfrey, cotoneasters, fuchsias, globe artichokes and cardoons, goldenrod, jasmines, knapweed, lavenders, mallows, Michaelmas daisies, raspberries, rhododendrons, thistles, vetches.

Bees are pretty as well as useful in every garden.

Delphiniums are one of the loveliest cottage garden bee plants.

Blue and lavender flowers are almost always good for bees. They certainly flock to the campanulas and Spanish lavender shown here.

Catnip or catmint (Nepeta) is one of the best bee plants and makes good groundcover, keeping the roots of this rose cool and moist.

Bluebells and pheasant's eye (Narcissus poeticus) naturalized in grass provide for bumble bees in spring; the grass can be cut later.

'Tydeman's White' and other flowering redcurrants underplanted with primroses buzz with bees on warm spring days.

Leeks and carrots left to flower attract many beneficial insects to the garden and are loved by bees and hoverflies.

Buddleia davidii 'Pink delight' smells sweet to bees, butterflies like this peacock, and people.

BUTTERFLY PLANTS

Buddleia, Sedum spectabile, goldenrod, valerian and lavendar are amongst the best attractants, also: *Dianthus, Hesperis, Hyssop,* lilacs, *Lonicera, Lychnis, Lythrum, Myositis, Origanum, Viola.*

PLANTS TO ATTRACT OTHER CREATURES

Bats eat tremendous numbers of flying pests and they are best encouraged by providing roosting and hibernating sites. Trees like limes which harbour large crops of aphids shower them off into the breeze and will attract bats.

Beetles are such a large group that they really need to be considered separately from insects – they are mostly friends, but particular exceptions are the strawberry and pollen beetles. To stop bigger predators spotting the useful ones, groundcover is essential, especially broad-leaved plants that collect dew or provide hiding places under leaves or rough bark. Leave bits of bark and dead wood around to hide beetles during the day.

Cats are much abused because of the free fertilizer packages they leave in seed-beds. However, there is nothing like a few cats for keeping the birds on their toes and decimating the rodent population. Keep cats about by planting catnip (*Nepeta mussinii* or *cataria*) and valerian in warm, sheltered corners.

Lavender attracts bees and butterflies, even cabbage whites.

Frogs and toads eat many pests; they need water and wet places to live. They will be keener to patrol the garden if there is good groundcover, preferably damp underneath. Keep a lush, moist, overgrown corner in the greenhouse and you can have them living and dining there.

Hedgehogs are well-known friends in the UK, but contrary to what many people believe they do not thrive on the traditional milk and bread – dogfood is a better treat! Plant dense-growing shrubs with dry centres for them to hibernate in – brambles and conifers, for example. Hedgehog boxes can be put underneath these shrubs or hedges: make them waterproof from above, at least 30 cm (1 ft) cubed with a 7.5–10 cm (3–4 in) entrance hole, and fill them with dry leaves.

There is even a predatory slug called Pestacella: it is yellowish with a small vestigial shell on the tail end. This eats other slugs, but is quickly killed by a diet of poisoned ones, so is now almost unknown.

PLANTS TO ATTRACT BIRDS

Of course many gardeners often wish to get rid of birds, but on the whole they are definitely beneficial. Individual crops may need to be protected if you encourage birds, but most of them control pests more than they spoil crops – the common sparrow and pigeons are notable exceptions. Habitat and food are important if you are to attract birds, but water is essential and like us birds appreciate a bath – somewhere the cat can't get at them. As soon becomes apparent to any gardener with a ripening crop, birds much prefer our cultivated fruit to the wild fare nature provides. Often they are just after the succulence, so the damage can be reduced by providing water for them to drink. The more fruit you grow the less damage your resident population can do, so plant sacrificial crops (see p. 33).

HOVERFLY PLANTS

The best plant to bring these in is the low-growing, self-sowing annual *Limnanthes douglasii*. This should be grown as much as possible, filling the garden with hoverflies and feeding bees. Buckwheat and *Convolvulus tricolor* are excellent at supplying nectar later in the season. Most flowers will help hoverflies, especially: *Alyssum, Arabis, Aubretia, Geranium* (but not *Pelargonium*), goldenrod, heliotrope, honesty, *Iberis*, all marigolds, Michaelmas daisies, all the mints, *Muscari, Nemophilia, Nicotiana, Petunia*, phlox, all poppies, *Sedum spectabile*, Shasta daisy, stock, sunflower, sweet rocket, sweet William, sweet Wivelsfield, wallflowers. Letting celeries and carrots go to seed will encourage hoverflies and other beneficial insects.

Pot marigolds are excellent hoverfly attractants and help protect these squash plants.

A luxuriant jungle creates a sheltered habitat in which many forms of life can live or hide.

PLANT COMPANIONS TO BIRDS: TREES AND SHRUBS

Amelanchiers are pretty trees covered in small fruits from midsummer.

Beech is excellent as a hedge as it provides good cover for nests and perches; during the winter it keeps its leaves, giving shelter.

Berberis is a genus of prickly plants with spiky leaves and thorns; it provides protection, shelter and berries. Conifers provide excellent nest sites, roosts and protection against bad weather.

Cornus mas, Cornelian cherry, is an edible fruit following abundant yellow flowers.

The *Crataegus* or thorn genus is beloved for nesting sites and berries.

Elaeagnus pungens is a dense evergreen, good for nesting places and protection against bad weather.

Elderberry is one of the very best for perches, nests and berries.

Holly is well known for dense evergreen growth and occasional berries.

Laurel is better for shelter than nesting as it is so easily climbed by predators.

Lonicera or honeysuckle species are not all climbers; some, like *L. purpussii* and *L. fragrantissima*, are shrubby – they are also winter flowering. The dense growth makes them good for nests and they berry freely.

Mahonias are related to *Berberis* and have holly-like leaves; the grape-like fruit is edible and birds love it.

Pyracantha or firethorn has horrible spines and loads of berries.

Shrub roses are impenetrable to predators and produce rosehips, so are of immense benefit for nesting sites and food.

Sorbus spp., the rowans and whitebeams, are renowned for plentiful berries.

Yew is one of the best nesting trees, as the vertical trunks are full of nooks and crannies hidden by ubiquitous evergreen shoots; birds love the berries though the seeds and foliage are poisonous.

This path through raised beds is just hard-packed soil.

PLANT COMPANIONS TO BIRDS: CLIMBERS AND WALL SHRUBS

Ceanothus is a not very hardy group of blue-flowered shrubs that need a wall for protection as much as for support. Because they are mostly evergreen and have dense growth, they make good nest sites.

Clematis romp everywhere and nests can be found all through them. The seeds of many have fine floss that can be used for nesting material.

Cotoneaster is a genus of shrubs that need a wall to fall against. They provide some nesting places, but are really cherished for their wealth of berries.

Garrya elliptica is an evergreen grown on walls for shelter. It gives dense cover for nests.

Hedera spp., the ivies, are well known for turning walls into thickets full of birds. They provide berries late in the year.

Hydrangea petiolaris is another climber which can become large and dense, but it is slower growing than the ivies.

Jasminum officinale is a sweet-scented summer climber that needs a warm spot; then it gives good nest sites. *Jasminum nudiflorum* is nearly evergreen, yellow-flowered in winter with denser, lower growth than the summer-scented variety.

Lonicera spp. are mostly climbers and almost all have glorious scents. They provide good nesting sites and berries for birds and require little attention.

Parthenocissus or Virginia creepers can cover acres of wall with nest sites and they also produce berries after hot summers.

Polygonum baldschuanicum and the closely related *P. aubertii*, the Russian vine or fleece flower, are capable of swamping an aircraft hangar. Good for covering eyesores and turning them into bird sanctuaries, they are for the larger garden only!

Roses are unclimbable and easy to fix nests on; later in the year they produce hips. Birds love them as much as people, so plant lots. The cultivar 'Kiftsgate' will cover a house. 'Souvenir de Claudius Denoyel' was host to seven nests in an old rectory garden I visited recently; it is also gloriously scented.

Wisteria is a good nest provider with the twisting stems producing many nooks and ledges.

This lovely arch of honeysuckle has three nests in it.

Roses make a cottage garden complete: see what happens when you cover the 'Albertine' rose with your hand in this picture of James and Maggie Lythgoe's garden.

SACRIFICIAL FRUIT AND VEGETABLE COMPANIONS WHICH WILL ATTRACT BIRDS

Apples are slaughtered by birds, so even if you plant as many of them as you can squeeze in, the fruit will still all be gone by the new year.

Blackberries are traditional nesting places and the cultivated berries yield far more than the wild.

Blackcurrants are not as popular with birds as redcurrants, but the berries still go.

Cherries disappear with great speed and large trees make good perching and places.

Gooseberries are eaten despite their thorns.

Grapes are good at producing berries and nesting sites, especially if they are allowed to ramble.

Loganberries are rarely seen ripe if they are unprotected.

Mulberries are slow to fruit, so it would be far-sighted and worthwhile to plant one for the birds to feed on while you rest underneath in your old age.

Peaches may go unrecognized on the trees for years, but as soon as one bird discovers them they all seem to learn.

Pears are rarely given the chance to ripen on the trees, let alone rot on the ground.

Plums hang on the ends of twigs and so sustain less damage than most fruit until they hit the ground; either way the wasps always get them.

Raspberries are one of the crops birds love most. The autumn-fruiting ones spread the season; yellow ones may go unscathed for a while, but not for long.

Redcurrants gain enormous benefit from a fruit cage – without a fruitcage or net you will have none left!

Strawberries are addictive to birds; they cannot get enough, so plant many varieties, with alpines and autumn croppers to spread the fruiting season.

Tayberries are a new, even more bird-palatable type of loganberry.

Whitecurrants are versions of redcurrants and do not disappear quite as fast.

Worcesterberries have dense, thorny growth and resemble gooseberries, but are larger plants with smaller berries, most suitable for wild corners.

When fruit fails to satisfy the birds' appetites you can sow some of the following vegetables for tasty little seedling snacks: Beet and its relatives are razored off as soon as they emerge. These include red and yellow beetroot, Swiss chard and leaf beet. They are the number one favourite snack in my garden, unfortunately.

Brassicas are popular with pigeons; other birds attack the small leaves, but once the plants are established they become too tough for most garden birds. Chickens love greens and if you let them in amongst the brassicas they choose cauliflower and broccoli leaves first.

Lettuces are a ready meal for birds until they bolt; then they become bitter, although chickens will still eat them. Pea seedlings are another popular snack when they are small; those that survive produce peas for the birds later.

Spinach rarely survives emergence unless it is protected.

Below: Redcurrants are possibly the easiest fruit to grow – and the most easily lost to birds.

Opposite: Cherries are almost as irresistible to birds as redcurrants.

A final word about attracting birds. Swallows and house martins bind their nests with mud and there is now a shortage as garden ponds rarely have muddy edges. Furthermore, there are fewer piles of strawy dung and less livestock leaving hair on hedges, which deprives house martins of the other material they need for their nests. They can make them of mud alone, but the nests then fall off when the mud bakes and shrinks with nothing strengthening it – so hang out hair trimmings and put bowls of mud by the pool edge to help these insect eaters.

Plants to attract people

People are also important visitors to the garden and can be encouraged: they will visit more often and stay longer if the habitat is sheltered and provided with resting places. It is impossible to make a sensible short list of attractive plants – the choice is just too vast, and anyway more depends on setting than intrinsic beauty. For many people scent is as important as colour. The best inducement is a well-spread table. Use fine herbs, good bread, fresh fruit and vegetables and you will never be short of guests or compliments.

A delightful spot that encourages one to linger. You cannot have too many in a garden.

This simple seat has wild strawberries underneath, perfectly happy in the dappled shade.

WATER, THE HIDDEN COMPANION

Most important of all for wildlife large or small is water. It is really the key to a garden, *the* basis of all life. It is the medium in which chemical and biological reactions take place, dissolving rock dusts and carrying products from micro-organisms to roots and vice versa. Water evaporating is the pump that lifts nutrients from the roots to the topmost leaf and then transports sugars produced by photosynthesis back to the roots. It makes up four-fifths of every plant.

Water will also lure and retain more different forms of life than any other attraction. Bird baths, waterfalls, fountains, a deep pond, a shallow pool, a muddy and stagnant ditch or just a sunk-in sink will all appeal to different creatures. Even jam jars or the like can play a useful role in providing water for small animals and birds.

Garden pools probably now account for the majority of breeding sites for frogs, toads and newts. (Derelict plots may supply many breeding places in the form of old basements, sinks and junk, but I am not suggesting that these be used as models.) The natural breeding places such as farm ponds have been filled in, ditches scraped clean or piped and marshlands drained.

My small pond is surrounded with a low fence of rotting logs, making a wonderful wildlife haven – and a seat from which one can sit and gaze. Although only a few years old it is full of life, especially newts; dragonflies buzz around and a grass snake visits.

We seem to be experiencing more droughts in recent years, so water must be guarded most carefully. Storing rainfall in tanks helps, but far more can be stored in the ground and in plants. Increasing the amount of humus in the soil raises its water-holding capacity enormously. Green manures, compost and minimal cultivation improve the soil's ability to store water falling in winter till the following summer when it is needed. Weeds are a quick way to lose moisture and should be eradicated from any area where water shortage may be a problem. A dust mulch used to be advocated as a means of conserving water, but it only works because it controls weeds at the same time.

A mulch on top of the soil is immensely more effective than a dust mulch at stopping the water in the soil evaporating. A mulch of shredded bark will retain as much as its own depth of rain, though coarser ones are less absorbent. A very absorbent mulch can be disadvantageous if there is only a little rainfall at a time. It will absorb each shower and prevent it reaching the soil; only heavy precipitation will penetrate through to the roots. This is why mulches are put on after rainy spells, not before.

Well-mulched bare soil loses water at the slowest possible rate with no plants taking any out, but grow only a few plants widely spaced out in hot, dry conditions and they will start to take out a lot of water to compensate. The more exposed they are, the more water they will absorb. Thus a few weeds take a lot of water from the soil and so do over-spaced crop plants. To minimize water loss with crops it is better to have them growing closer together, intermixed with companion plants. The microclimate formed by the mixed layers of leaves traps moisture-laden air; the leaves thus keep themselves and the soil moister and cooler, and at night more dew condenses.

The same occurs with deeper swards of grass and clover mixtures – these attract more dew than closely cropped grass. If the sward is allowed to grow up and tumble over it loses less water than if it is regularly cut long, but then there is less material being returned to the soil as fertility.

Orchard management in the days before herbicides was to keep grass cut regularly until after midsummer; then it would be allowed to grow long. The growing grass would take up free nutrients, particularly nitrogen, causing the fruit to ripen better. The long grasses falling over would use less moisture, leaving more to swell the crop. The long grass would then cushion and hide windfalls. In the fruit cage mulches are nearly essential as soft fruits need plentiful moisture and they are swelling during the drier days of midsummer. Many of the fungus problems to which soft fruits are prone – especially mildews – are aggravated if not actually caused by the bushes getting too dry at the roots and/or stagnant air around overcrowded tops. Sprinkling or spraying them with only a little water is worse than leaving them alone, as it increases the stress and makes them more vulnerable to disease. The same applies to other woodland plants, and especially to roses.

Wet gardens are best enjoyed from the shelter of a summerhouse or potting shed, as you can do a lot of damage by moving about in them. When it is wet plants are more succulent and young growths snap more easily; the soil is packed underfoot, breaking fine roots and excluding air.

Berberis atropurpurea, 'Silver posie' thyme, cotton lavender (Santolina) and Salix helvetica fill the ground, forming a dense cover of foliage which catches dew and keeps the soil cool and moist.

Later during dry periods the footprints evaporate water more rapidly than loose soil, while the hard surface forms clods.

The worst problem of wet gardens is that touching plants spreads and lets in diseases. Many of these wait for wet periods to release spores so that they can be carried in drops of water. Bacteria can similarly travel protected from the danger of desiccation. Research on the ways viruses enter leaves has shown that they find it difficult to penetrate existing wounds as the defence systems are repairing damage. The easiest way for them to attack healthy leaves was shown to be if the leaf was wetted with contaminated water and lightly rubbed. Deep wounds were less damaging as they stimulated more defence mechanisms. The moral is clear – walking among wet plants and particularly running their leaves through your fingers is probably doing them a great deal of harm. Bigger yields and more vigour can be gained more emphatically by one generous application of water at the right stage than by almost any other improvement you can make to reasonable growing conditions. Obviously poor conditions like low light or compacted soil need improving beforehand, but once the general conditions are favourable a single substantial watering can be more effective than any fertilizer. Crops whose seeds we eat, such as peas and beans, need copious water when they are in flower. Potatoes also respond best to water when they are in flower, as the flowering indicates that the little tubers are just beginning to swell. Saladings and leaf crops should have plenty of water throughout their lives. Rainwater is more valuable than tap water and every drop should be captured. Dead freezers make neat – and free – water butts.

Without sufficient water no life processes take place. Add some water and plants grow. Add plentiful water at the right time and they flourish.

This magnificent show of somewhat tender plants in pots relies on absolutely meticulous watering to keep it flourishing.

Water in any form adds interest and life to a garden.

Chapter 4

USING PLANT COMPANIONS

PLANNING YOUR GARDEN

Planning and taking time to consider the possible effects of each change are really the most important parts of any job, the more so with gardening when results can take a very long time to appear! If you have the luxury of planning a garden from scratch, a year spent observing a prospective garden will allow a much more effective plan to be drawn up. If the garden is put down to grass preparatory to making beds and borders, then a dry spell will show where the soil is moister and any geometric brown patches can disclose old foundations and pathways. This can save an incredible amount of wasted time and effort.

The best way to draw up a plan is to start by marking in those things that can't be easily changed – boundaries, buildings, solid paths, pipes, big trees and so on. Next, consideration needs to be given to future building plans – it is a terrible waste to put effort into a piece of ground that is going to disappear under a garage in a couple of years.

Choosing what you are to grow and in what quantity is a task to be undertaken with all the precision of a military exercise. It is not difficult to change the proportions of bedding plants, potatoes or cabbages if you find you have miscalculated, but the wrong mixture of apples or plums can be disastrous.

This in turn affects other decisions. For example, if you want a number of different sorts of apple in a small garden, you will have to grow them as cordons instead of as bushy trees. Cordons need support and are grown on wires, which need to be carried on posts; this then becomes a fence. To prevent it creating too much shade it is best if the cordon runs north-south, and this decision affects other parts of the design such as access and pathways. (In a large garden it is possible to have greater variety without too much extra work, as the simpler training of bushy trees takes less time than for the same number of cordons, and they produce more.)

The same applies to other areas of the garden. It is hard to make one flowerbed attractive all the year round, especially if it is crammed full of things that all flower in the spring. Several beds, carefully positioned, with emphasis on different seasons, can be better aesthetically and easier to maintain. Do not make them too small, though, or they will look bitty.

When the plan is decided and each area provisionally allocated, then and only then should trees be planted – they are slow to come into crop and detest being moved. Soft fruit and shrubs take next longest to mature, while herbs, vegetables and herbaceous plants are very quick and easy so can be left till last. To prevent competition, companion plantings should only be added when the main planting is well established.

This 'Improved Fertility' pear is trained on wires and posts flanking the vegetable beds which also run north–south.

88

Each smaller area of the garden should be looked at in the same way as the whole, putting in the permanent fixtures first, then the trees and shrubs. Once these are settled you can start to put in the softer-growing plants. But be patient. It is important to allow the woody plants to get going before the others are introduced. For optimum growth, a tree needs minimum competition (i.e. weed-free conditions) for upwards of two years and at least 2 m (6 ft) from the tree in every direction. Take time to build up the layers in this way so that no single one dominates.

Patience is the most important virtue where gardening is concerned, especially as the benefits of organic methods in general and of companion planting in particular are slow to have their full effect. It takes many seasons for predator populations to build up, for the soil to become healthier and for plants to grow strongly.

For the best quality plants, go to a specialized nursery, preferably a privately owned one, not part of a chain. This may mean you have to order by post. Order your plants well before you need them to ensure that you get the best selection and that they arrive before it is too late to plant them. The extra cost of delivery is a worthwhile expense as the choice of plants will be better and mail-order plants are often less expensive over all than those from garden centres.

Paths and drives

These are often the source of problems: unsuitable paths make a lot of work. Narrow grass pathways between lots of little beds mean there is a tremendous amount of edging to maintain. To reduce this, wherever possible paths and drives should have solid or concrete edges or be flanked by beds and borders. Gravel or pebbled paths next to grass mean stones in the lawnmower and grass growing into the paths. Surplus gravel drifting on to the soil from a path can easily be mixed in so that it disappears, while soil overflowing on to the gravel is untidy, so make gravel paths stand proud. Lavender, box or rosemary edging will suppress weeds and grow over the edge, saving a lot of work.

Solid paths are needed near the house and anywhere else that wear is heavy. Gravel paths should be separated from the house by some solid path or bits will be carted indoors. Grass paths are fine where wear is light, but if they are used frequently they will become bald in the middle, then unpleasant in the wet. A row of sunken stepping stones is the answer.

Be considerate of your plants: a path can get much hotter than bare soil, so grow plants that will not mind near it. Choose Mediterranean herbs with pleasant scents like thyme and lavender that can spill on to the path. Alternatively a path in the shade can be a cool, moist root run for plants such as Clematis which appreciate these conditions.

In between vegetable beds, the best paths are made of crushed gravel. This discourages slugs and snails, stays dry underfoot and is not very expensive. Sharp sand is excellent and can either be incorporated into the soil or just topped up when it becomes dirty. Bare soil needs more weeding, but is considerably cheaper than the rest. Stepping stones are a good compromise amongst vegetables or ornamentals.

Solid paths give the best working surface, but can be visually brutal. Here they are softened by geraniums and helianthemums.

Straw paths are fine as long as new straw is available – if it runs out, many flushes of weeds follow. Straw is pleasant to work from but soon gets dirty, blows in the wind and harbours pests. In the fruit cage straw paths become much more practical. Pine needles and bark materials make good paths, especially among shrubs or in woodland settings, and they inhibit slugs and weeds. They are pleasant to walk on but difficult to keep tidy, as like most mulches they are kicked about by birds.

GIVING PLANTS ENOUGH SPACE

Plants need enough space to grow in and where many of the same type are to be fitted in they need arranging in a pattern. You may prefer an irregular formation for aesthetic reasons, but in general rows or blocks are more efficient. This is most obvious in the vegetable plot. In the UK we tend to prefer row planting, though elsewhere blocks are as common or more so.

Plants grow better in blocks than in long, straight rows. The leaves meet and form a micro-environment underneath; this retains moisture and excludes weeds. The total space required for a given crop in blocks is less than for rows, as little room is needed for paths. Unless you want enormous specimens, the recommended distance apart for plants grown in rows is also about the best spacing for block planting.

Blocks may just consist of several short rows or they may form a specific pattern, such as square planting. This is most convenient for getting machinery between the plants – in commercial orchards, say – but the plants are not equal distances from those around them and the alleys can allow severe draughts.

Triangular planting means the rows are staggered so that the gap in one is blocked in the next, but the distances between each plant are not necessarily equal. If every plant is the same distance from each neighbour, like cells in a honeycomb, then it becomes hexagonal planting and this gives exactly the same area of ground to each. The advantage of this is that the leaf canopy and roots utilize both air and soil more efficiently. The total that can be planted into any area is 15 per cent higher for hexagonal planting than for square.

The onions on the nearest bed are planted too close together and are stunted; on the next bed, with wider spacing, they are bigger. Generally, it is preferable to have slightly smaller onions, as they keep better, but if they have been too crowded in a bed they will be good only for pickling.

Quincunx planting is similar to square planting but an extra plant is inserted in the middle of each square. This form is often used in orchards with the extra being a different, short-lived filler, removed as the main crop matures. On a smaller scale this is one way of fitting in companion plants or intercropping vegetables with low, quick-growing fillers such as lettuce between the main crop plants.

More complicated interplantings can follow similar lines, but care must be taken not to crowd and choke the main crop.

Block planting is not restricted to the productive garden: most ornamental plants also look much better when grouped together rather than mixed in singly. A bed composed of singletons or dot plants often just looks bitty, but group the plants in threes, fives and sevens and they will have more impact and reinforce each other. However, be careful not to make any ornamental plan too regimented unless that is the effect you want to achieve. If you want a very natural effect, say with drifts of bulbs in woodland, take the bulbs, or use stones to represent plants, scatter them blindly within the appointed area and plant them where they land.

SHELTER

This is most important in windswept localities but it is advantageous to increase shelter in parts of most gardens. A warm, snug corner will shield a few flowers to feed beneficial insects when it is howling with gales. Tender plants can be cosseted by surrounding them with tougher, taller plants and if harsh winds are thus kept off they may well survive colder weather. Be particularly careful about hardening off any plants you have been growing under cover – more transplants are damaged by windburn than by frost.

Building up hedges and screens of plants against cold winds benefits the whole garden, as they have a filtering effect which extracts heat from the wind; this then warms the plants. Yields are increased by nearly one sixth in fields with good hedges compared to those without and the same benefit can be gained in gardens. Hedges and screens are more effective than walls or solid fences which do not filter the wind but force it into gusts and eddies. If a wall or solid fence exists put trellis on top of it and grow climbers over it to gain some advantage.

Jerusalem artichokes make a quick shelter, growing way above head height by midsummer. They may need staking or tying together in windy areas. The flowering varieties are loved by insects, especially bees; the tubers are edible and prolifically produced.

Lamium galeobdolon 'Variegatum', one of the
deadnettle genus, is one of the most effective
weed-suppressing groundcover plants, but even
so this pretty little honesty has managed to raise
a purple flowerhead.

GROUNDCOVER CROPS AND 'LAWNS'

Groundcover plants may be ornamentals, but they have other uses too.
Groundcover stops soil erosion and leaching and prevents weeds
establishing themselves. It can produce plant material for use elsewhere, as
a green manure might. If you choose your groundcover plants carefully,
you can ensure that they do not compete with the main planting and that
they have other beneficial effects such as attracting bees.

Almost every suitable, and some not quite so suitable, plant has been
recommended as groundcover by someone trying to boost sales. Some
ludicrous suggestions are made, despite all common sense to the contrary.
Anyone who recommends roses as a groundcover needs their scruples
testing – they cannot have given a thought to anything beyond their cash
desk. Roses are wonderful plants in the right place, but not as sheets of
groundcover – trying to weed or extract litter from a bed of electrified
barbed wire could be fun by comparison!

The better groundcovers are companion plants using different soil layers
and light requirements to the main plants. They should also provide for
the other life in the garden and not require too much management. No
groundcover eliminates weeding and it adds to the difficulty in the early
years. Do not believe blandishments to the contrary – even mint beds will
still have some weeds appearing.

I find the best groundcover of all is the alpine strawberry. It tolerates
most situations; it flowers almost from last frost to first frost, benefiting
many insects; it is not invasive, but is tough, hardy and low-growing and
produces a useful fruit. The only drawback is that it is short-lived and
needs replanting every five or six years. Fortunately birds will spread
seeds and thus replacements about the garden. Ordinary strawberries also
make good groundcover but are not so accommodating and may harbour
virus diseases.

The following suggested groundcover plants are chosen because they
attract beneficial insects or bees and are tough and simple to propagate.

Ivy makes good groundcover for beetles and small predators, and the honesty can struggle through to provide nectar for beneficial insects.

Alchemilla mollis Lady's mantle Zones 4–8. Height 45 cm (18 in). Will grow in sun or shade and is very tough. Attracts beneficial insects.

Ajuga reptans Bugleweed Zones 3–9. Height 15 cm (6 in). Very vigorous purple or green plant for damp areas, but requires good drainage to prevent rot in hot, humid summers. Its long flowering period is good for bumble bees.

Matricaria recutita and *Chamaemelum nobile* (also known as *Anthemis nobilis*) Respectively German chamomile (an annual) and lawn or Roman chamomile (a perennial, hardy to zone 4). Height 30 cm (12 in). Both make beautifully scented cover crops that provide material for stimulating compost. They benefit plants and insects, but need sun.

Cotoneaster spp. Some hardy to zone 4. Heights vary from 20 cm (8 in) to 5 m (16 ft) – be careful which species you choose! Rapidly spreading shrubs, superb for bees in flower and birds in fruit as well as providing wildlife cover.

Geranium spp. Hardiest kinds to zone 3. Height 45 cm (18 in). These are the cranesbills, not the *Pelargonium* houseplants. They are tough, cope with sun or shade and are beneficial to insects.

Hedera helix English ivy Zones 5–9. Can grow to 10 m (32 ft) if supported; otherwise spreads vigorously as groundcover. Even in heavy shade it provides good wildlife cover and is especially useful to bees as it flowers so late in the year.

Lavandula spp. Lavender Hardiest types zones 6–9. Height 60 cm (2 ft). Attractive to many beneficial insects as well as to us. Good at suppressing weeds, but needs full sun and good drainage, particularly in damp climates.

Limnanthes douglasii Poached egg plant or meadow foam Height 30 cm (12 in). A self-seeding annual and one of the best cover crops, especially under roses, shrubs and fruit. Attracts bees and beneficial insects in staggering numbers.

Mentha spp. Mints Hardiest types to zone 3. Height up to 1.2 m (4 ft)! All the mints are vigorous, so should only be put where they can be contained by concrete or paths. They like moist conditions but will tolerate shade and are very beneficial.

Thymus spp. Thyme Height 30 cm (1 ft). There are many varieties, some hardy to zones 4 or 5 and all good for bees and other insects. One of the most attractive of all groundcover plants.

Trifolium spp. Clovers Height 30–60 cm (12 in–2 ft). The low- growing clovers such as the annual crimson or the perennial white (zone 3) are not just good nitrogen-fixing groundcover, they are also very beneficial to bees and other insects. Clovers provide cover for ground beetles, are hosts to predators of the woolly aphis and help deter cabbage root fly if sown underneath cabbages. They dislike henbane and may stimulate deadly nightshade into germination.

For really difficult or larger areas try:

Cerastium tomentosum Snow-in-summer Zones 2–7. Height 8 cm (3 in). Invasive, but will tolerate dry conditions.

Galeobdolon luteum Yellow archangel Zones 4–9. Height 1 m (3 ft). A *Lamium* with yellow flowers. Shade tolerant and beneficial to insects, but very invasive.

Erica and *Calluna* spp. Heathers and lings Some hardy to zones 3 or 4. Various heights. These seem to be ever popular, despite the fact that many of them are difficult to establish in lime soils, however many bags of irreplaceable peat you incorporate. That said, they are very tough once established and prevent weeds from germinating underneath them. They do poorly in hot climates.

Hypericum calcynum Rose of Sharon Zones 6–9. Height up to 1.5 m (5 ft), but usually shorter; spreads well. Tough, but not very beneficial.

Sedum acre Zones 3–8. Height 2.5–5 cm (1–2 in). This is poisonous to humans, but useful because it will grow almost anywhere, even in very dry positions. The flowers attract insects and the plant is believed to be beneficial as a cover for *Clematis* roots.

Vinca spp. Periwinkles Height up to 45 cm (18 in). Too invasive and loose growing to be recommended almost anywhere other than rampantly wild woodland. *V. major*, zones 7-9, is more vigorous than *V. minor*, zones 4–9.

Lawns and Turf Care

Grass is almost the ideal groundcover as it can be aesthetically pleasing and produce tremendous amounts of fertility-enhancing clippings. Be careful to establish plants well before letting grass near them, as it competes vigorously!

If any area of ground is cut regularly, rough growths and weeds will eventually turn into grass sward. This process is speeded up by oversowing with better grasses and adding in clovers. Putting back the clippings builds up fertility and the regular cut slowly converts the population into less pernicious mixtures of plants. If and when the time comes to break up the ground (see p. 152), it will require much less work to produce clean soil and establish the new beds than would have been needed before the grass had its effect.

Maintenance cutting should be done every week throughout the growing season and care should be taken not to cut too close. A height of 4–6 cm (1–2 in) is ideal; anything shorter causes the grass to brown off and mosses to increase. Longer grass is healthier than short and outcompetes weeds and moss more easily. If the clippings are returned to the lawn after alternate cuts, the fertility improves, helping to produce more clippings so that a surplus can be taken for use as a mulch elsewhere.

After several seasons of cutting, strong-growing perennial grasses will outcompete most other plants. Clovers will survive as long as the grass is not cut too short, so its seed can be oversown at the same time as the grass seed. For a uniform appearance it is easier to sow clover everywhere than to try and eradicate the odd patches. Sow sweet white or red clover as companions to grasses and encourage them with lime and by cutting the sward higher; this keeps the turf green longer in dry weather. Clovers are helped by cutting higher; closer cropping encourages first daisies then moss. A mix of red clover and alsike (the white- or pink-flowered variety) is more effective than either alone at improving yields of grass or hay.

Most of the other common lawn weeds are no problem and merely add variety, they are natural companions and disappear as conditions change. They become less evident when the grass is growing strongly; rosette weeds may persist, but plantains and thistles are not difficult to eradicate by hand or with a sharp knife.

Mosses are only a problem in short grass and, like the weeds, are choked out in long, lush swards. They prefer acid conditions, so adding lime discourages them. As turf tends to become acid, even on alkaline soils, annual liming will nearly always be of great benefit, simultaneously adding to the fertility and suppressing undesirable acid lovers.

The presence of daisies suggests that the turf needs to be limed and that the cutting height is set too low. Creeping buttercups are a sign of even greater acidity and more need for liming; they might also indicate poor drainage and a compacted soil. Buttercups (Ranunculaceae) are fond of wet, acid conditions, so draining and liming discourages them. They secrete toxins that inhibit clovers, thus depriving the grass.

When sowing grass remember that the fine, expensive grasses like acid soils and can be cut very close, but do not resist weeds, moss or wear. The tougher grasses prefer lime in the soil, resist wear, weeds and moss, but cannot be cut as close. Some chamomile, creeping thyme, yarrow, daisies and pennyroyal will make the sward prettier and sweetly scented. If you really like hand weeding then you can make a lawn from Roman chamomile, *Chamaemelum nobile*. Use the creeping variety 'Treneague', propagated from root cuttings. For orchards, meadows and longer sward a small proportion of alfalfa, clover, mustard, nettles, vetch or yarrow will be beneficial.

Grass is the perfect backdrop, especially for this pink rose 'Zéphirine drouhin'.

Chapter 5

THE ORNAMENTAL GARDEN

Although this book is mainly about the way plants grow together, the primary concern of most gardeners is to create attractive and tranquil gardens for pleasure. Ornamental plants can be combined with food plants (and more will be said about this in the next chapter), but for the reasons discussed in Chapter 2 we usually end up with a division between flowers and produce. We may then group plants within the ornamental garden for our convenience or because of their own needs. Because most herbs come originally from the Mediterranean region, they benefit from a sunnier climate than the UK normally provides, so they tend to be grouped in the same hot, dry bed. Plants for herbaceous borders go together because of their habit of growth; so do shrubs, and alpines are happiest on a well-drained artificial scree.

That said, we choose plants for the flower garden largely because of beauty or scent. We thus have to consider how plants look together as well as whether or not they will do well in given combinations or conditions, and this chapter considers some common subdivisions of the ornamental garden with a view to achieving an aesthetically pleasing result without sacrificing good planting.

THE COLOUR GARDEN

Probably the commonest desire in any ornamental area is to have plenty of bright colour – nothing gladdens the heart more than masses of harmonious tones.

However, just massing colours together can be overpowering rather than pleasing. Bedding plants are some of the most oppressed plants in our gardens, forced into companionship with no thought given to their needs or preferences (or to colour combinations – I swear some gardeners are either colour blind or malicious!). Harmony is very important and although strong clashes of colour can occasionally be effective, it is generally more acceptable to have sympathetic colours next to each other, often in muted hues of the same pastel shades. These can be slowly modified along a bed or border to give a wide spread of colours, but keeping strongly contrasting ones far apart.

If you don't trust your own colour sense, try some of the combinations on the following pages:

Colour harmony is the attraction here: the greys and purples mingle beautifully with the Rosa mundi *and* Rosa gallica *bushes.*

Muscari and *Ficaria verna* The blue of the grape hyacinth coupled with the yellow of the celandines gladdens the heart in early spring. The grape hyacinth leaves appear in August and hardly compete with those of the celandine, which do not come until late winter. Autumn crocus, whose leaves appear in spring but flowers stand alone in September can be usefully added to this combination.

Dianthus and *Nepeta* Pinks or carnations go well in front of catnip, which provides a muted backdrop for their pastel shades. They all tolerate dry, chalky spots.

Lilies grown up through skimmias or daphnes benefit from the support of the shrubs which rarely grow too tall for them and protect the young shoots from frost or treading. The lily leaves blend well with those of the shrubs and their flowers add a further period of interest. As the shrubs have small pale flowers the lilies can add a touch of flamboyance with large bright blooms in yellow, red or orange; the divinely scented regal lily (*Lilium regale*) is more subtle and refined for a quiet place.

Sweet rocket and double white lilac look fantastic together. Both need rich soil to do well and the sweet rocket hides the often too bare lower limbs of the lilac.

Nerine bulbs grown up through lavender benefit from the support and winter protection the shrub gives them. The pink flowers of the nerines are shown to best advantage against the mauve-grey foliage in autumn.

Lavender, *Santolina* and *Sedum spectabile* grown together provide a dense, weed-excluding cover with delectable shades of grey and green that is remarkably constant through the seasons and can make an excellent sheltering backdrop or foil for small plants or bulbs in front.

Dianthus and Nepeta, *pinks and catnip, go well together and thrive in dry, chalky spots.*

Jasminum stephanense on *Eucalyptus gunni* looks gorgeous. The early foliage of the jasmine is brightest yellow with hints of red and contrasts brilliantly with the steely blue of the *Eucalyptus* which is supported and constrained by the climber.

Chives or garlic and roses are a classic combination, benefiting the rose by protecting it from fungal disease and pest attacks and hiding the bare lower framework. As the alliums die down in winter the rose can still benefit from heavy mulching.

Thyme or catnip (*Nepeta*) benefit roses by keeping the roots cool, moist and shaded. They hide the bare lower framework and provide another season of interest with their flowers; these in turn attract beneficial insects which can reduce the incidence of pest attacks on the roses.

Cyclamen and *Hedera*. Ivy is good groundcover but dull. Cyclamens have similar but more attractive marbled foliage, so tend to go unnoticed until their flowers appear – then this combination is magical.

Primroses and flowering redcurrant come out together and look superb; Tydeman's white flowering redcurrant makes the combination serene and regal. In either case the shrub allows enough early light through to the primrose leaves for them to survive; in return the primroses suppress weeds.

Violets are natural understorey woodland plants and go well beneath daphnes and other deciduous shrubs which allow early spring light to filter through to them; in return, the violets prevent weeds from gaining a foothold.

Bluebells (*Endymion*) with *Mahonia* make a fabulous combination of blue and yellow; the bluebells suppress weeds beneath the shrubs.

Rosemary and *Helichrysum angustifolium* have similar foliage but while the former is green, the latter is grey, so they contrast beautifully. Both need a dry, sunny spot in order to do well.

Roses and peonies both require rich, moist soil. The roses need to be grown as standards to raise their heads above the clumps of peonies. Take care that the colours do not clash – whites and pinks go best together and look good with the rich green foliage of the peonies.

Roses, lavender and *Fuchsia riccatonii* or *magellanica* make another good combination with a long season of flower interest. The low-growing lavender makes a foil for the others and protects the fuchsia's roots over winter.

Right: *These lilies are growing up through a* Daphne odora *'Aureo-marginata', which protects their young buds and supports their stems. In return, the lilies cast a light shade back over the daphne in midsummer.*

Something that is often overlooked is the value of shades of green. Leaf colour varies tremendously and contrasting foliage can be every bit as effective as striking flower colour – and it is easier to achieve. A solid mass of various greens makes a sympathetic backdrop for the flowers and helps even out strong hues. What is more, foliage has a much longer season of interest than most flowers. Combining different foliage forms can produce an elaborate and impressive result. Spiky or large leaves give a tropical feel, delicate filigree can be set against a darker evergreen, and of course there is a whole range of species with purple, yellow, silver or variegated leaves to add yet more interest. Almost any mixture of foliage can benefit from the addition of white flowers, as they have a similar soothing effect to the combinations of greens.

Almost any pleasing combination is better than monoculture, as it increases the range and diversity of plants; this then encourages a wider spread of life living on and about them, creating a more stable ecosystem that will resist pests and diseases. There are thousands upon thousands of different plants to choose from if you wish to create themes or plays of colour. Be warned, though – it may be better not to insist on growing say an all white, all red or all blue-flowered border. Going to these extremes might entail forcing plants from too many different backgrounds together for their comfort. Remember, the individual needs of every single plant must be met if they are to do well.

Foliage can be spectacular, as with this cardoon.

THE SILVER GARDEN

One of the most visually pleasing themes is the white or silver garden where all the plants have white flowers or white or silver foliage. In practice other flower colours creep in and can be effective amongst the serenity of silver, grey and green shades. Many Mediterranean plants have grey or silver foliage as protection against hot, dry conditions so in northern Europe they need dry, warm sheltered gardens. This makes them ideal for patios and terraces. Stone or brick benches, solid or stone paths, walls and statuary will help retain warmth, and a fountain or pool will also add to the southern ambience.

Other good plants for this garden are *Santolina incana*, the lavenders *Lavandula spica*, *L. stoechas* or *L. pedunculata*, *Perovskia*, *Stachys lanata*, *Helichrysum angustifolium*, *Rosmarinus*, *Cistus*, *Helianthemum*, *Artemisia*, especially *A. abrotanum*, *Cerastium tomentosum*, *Dianthus*, *Senecio greyii*, *Crambe cordifolia* and *Sempervivum arachnoideum*.

Unfortunately, many silver plants suffer in the hot, humid climate of the eastern US where the leaf hairs hold too much moisture. This leads to leaf and crown rots. Some are more resistant than others, including the taller *artemisias*. Good drainage and air circulation are the best ways of preventing these rots.

Snow-in-summer (Cerastium tomentosum) *is ideal for warm, sunny banks or rockeries, and enjoys the heat thrown up by a brick or stone path. It makes excellent groundcover, but is very vigorous, so be careful not to let it choke out other plants.*

THE SCENTED GARDEN

Perfume, like colour, is very much a matter of taste. There are scented flowers and foliage in every form and colour imaginable, yet many gardens have so few. They are often scented for the benefit of insects, not people, and so are good at bringing in and breeding up pests and predators. Scented annuals can be used to fill almost any bare spot; biennials and bulbs have to be planned in with the overall design.

Annuals
Without doubt sweet peas have one of the loveliest scents; the old-fashioned kinds with few flowers on a stem are the best.

Night-scented stock (*Matthiola longipetala*) is intoxicating and I sow it often each year. It looks better mixed with Virginia stocks (*Malcolmia maritima*), which are almost scentless but prettier than the dingy night-scented variety. Ten-week stocks (also *Matthiola*) are bigger and sturdier with all-day scent.

Nicotiana, the half-hardy night-scented tobaccos, are wonderful, filling a garden in the evening.

Gilia tricolor has a pretty little flower and a unique, penetrating scent.

Sweet Alyssum (*Lobularia maritima* or *Alyssum maritimum*) is honey- scented according to many people, but it makes others think of cats.

Mignonette (*Reseda*), *Mentzelia*, nasturtium (*Tropaeolum*), *Phacelia* and *Scabiosa* are annuals whose scent I love.

Biennials
Everyone should grow wallflowers (*Cheiranthus cheiri*) for spring cheer.

Brompton stocks (*Matthiola incana*) are magnificently opulent in scent and form.

Sweet rocket (*Hesperis matronalis*) is not often grown but resembles a tall stock.

A glorious display of sweet peas: summer is not summer without them.

Sweet Williams are well-known *Dianthus* hybrids, but try also the more delicate Sweet Wivelsfield.

Bulbs
These can be planted almost everywhere but can then make weeding tiresome. They are very useful to insects as many flower early in year.

Hyacinths (zones 4–9) can have an almost overpowering scent.

Bluebells (*Endymion*, zones 3–9) are more pleasant and grape hyacinths (*Muscari*, zones 5-8) are sweet.

Regal lilies (*Lilium regale*, zones 3–8) are so powerfully scented later in the year that they can be smelt a long way off. These are easy to grow from seed and should be in every garden.

Abyssinian gladiolus (*Acidanthera murielae*, zones 8–10) is an unusual white form with a delicate sweetness. It is not easy to grow in the UK, but thrives in warmer climates, including much of the US. In zones where this plant is not hardy, the bulbs are easily stored dry, indoors.

The Patio and Loggia: ideal for a herb garden

The area nearest the house is usually warm, dry and sheltered and suits a silver theme as suggested above. Herbs do particularly well here, and it's handy to have them near the kitchen. A loggia or pergola can create privacy and shelter at the same time, and blends the house and the garden together aesthetically. As this is an important place, the plants here need be chosen as much for scent as for appearance.

Never be without rosemary, thyme (especially *T. herba barona*), sage, Bowles' apple mint (*Mentha rotundifolia*), basil in every possible variety and the unbelievably delicious true lemon verbena (*Lippia* or *Aloysia citriodora*, zones 8–10), which is almost hardy in much of the UK. Any of the following will add pleasurable scents to the air when you brush against them: bergamot (*Monarda*), chamomile, the curry plant (*Helichrysum angustifolium*, zones 7–9), fennel, feverfew, hyssop, lavenders, marjoram, mints, rue, southernwood and even wormwood. Plant them liberally. Clary sage is short-lived but will please you and many, many insects.

When you run out of space, go up: roses have lovely scents and the climbers are the most powerful. Jasmine is obligatory in my opinion, as are the honeysuckles, of which there are many different varieties almost all with wonderful perfumes.

Feverfew, especially the golden form Chrysanthemum parthenium *'Aureum', seen here against a backdrop of phlox, is ideal at the front of borders: it is tough, grows practically anywhere and gives off a pleasant scent when you brush against it.*

Plants in pots need regular watering, but one great advantage to compensate for this is that they can be moved inside for winter display or protection in harsh weather.

Passionflowers (*Passiflora incarnata*, zones 6–9, *P. caerulea*, zones 8–10) are hardier and more scented than most people imagine, *Wisteria* (zones 4–9) also hides a scent and so do many *Clematis*. Some *Clematis montana*, including 'Elisabeth', and the almost hardy *C. armandii* (zones 8–9) are delightful, but *C. flammula* (zones 6–9), the fragrant virgin's bower, is the sweetest and most poetic. The sweet autumn clematis (*C.maximowicziana*, zones 4–9) is similar and widely grown in the eastern US. Many rarities such as *Akebia quinata* (zones 4–9), *Cytisus battandieri* (zones 7–9) and *Trachelospermum jasminoides* (zones 8–10) are worth pursuing.

Wherever possible, grow your plants in the ground, unless you deliberately want to restrict the growth of a rampant species. They will invariably grow better, winter more successfully and live longer. Pots, window boxes and planters confine the root growth, can only contain limited nutrients and expose the plant to extreme fluctuations of moisture and temperature. They also require you to spend a lot of time watering. If you have to use containers, use the biggest possible, fill them with a rich compost and choose tough plants such as thymes, lavender, rosemary and summer bedding.

THE HERBACEOUS BORDER

Most plants chosen for the herbaceous border die back annually and the top growth is then best cut only two thirds back after it has all withered. This allows the plants to reabsorb nutrients into their roots for the next year. Do not raze them to the ground or there will be no protection for the young shoots.

Much was said in Chapter 2 about how these plants came together, pretty well regardless of their preferences for sun/shade, acid/lime, wet/dry, etc, and how they have now been selected for compatibility and beneficial effect. One of the commonest plants found in herbaceous schemes is the Shasta daisy *Chrysanthemum* x *superbum*; but it gives off inhibiting root secretions and the cut flowers are well known for causing others to wilt. This plant needs lots of space as it will outcompete almost anything. If a garden is let go, it will probably be the last survivor.

The Shasta daisy is a member of the Compositae family, many of which use exudations against pests and diseases. *Chrysanthemum coccineum* is effective at killing nematodes. The flowers of *C. cinerariafolium* and *C. roseum* have been powdered for two thousand years for use as an insect killer. The commercial version, pyrethrum, is used in massive amounts because of its very low toxicity to mammals.

Lupins also feature in most herbaceous borders. They are well known for suppressing germination around them; they also add to soil fertility. Many varieties are poisonous, but those that are not make a very useful green manure. They improve soil texture and are generally beneficial, supporting vast populations of aphids and thus predators after flowering. Noted since classical times for their ability to suppress weeds, especially fat hen, they are hindered by the presence of buckwheat but stimulate its growth. Not only are they leguminous, providing nitrogen, but their root secretions unlock reserves of phosphates that would otherwise be inaccessible to most plants.

Borders of lavender, box or rosemary will prevent the invasion of slugs and snails. Growing marigolds and any of the pungent herbs will help confuse pests and encourage beneficial insects. Marigolds (the *Tagetes* genus) may have been selected for their colours and probably also unconsciously for the part they play in keeping other plants healthier. They may and should be grown widely in as many parts of the garden as they can be squeezed into. French or African marigolds, originally from South America, are useful half-hardy annuals. Much research has been done into their ability to kill nematodes and this is now beyond dispute. The Mexican form *T. minuta* is most effective and also chokes weeds, even bindweed. They are all hosts to hoverflies and also discourage wireworms, millipedes and other soil pests.

Pot marigolds (*Calendula officinalis*) are self-seeding hardy annuals whose flowers are used in soups and salads. In the garden they are beneficial to many insects and plants as they supposedly repel dogs from their vicinity and attract hoverflies.

Herbaceous plants are not often scented, though lily of the valley (*Convallaria*) is divine and some of the peonies have scents that on dew-wetted mornings seem to have come from heaven. Some members of the *Hosta* and *Hemerocallis* genera have delicious scents, though they are not generally known for it. Evening primrose and the true primrose, cowslips, violets and pinks are all too well perfumed to exclude. Phlox has a strange, evocative aroma, a subtle blend of sweet and musty.

Spurge, Polygonum bistorta, *red campion, aquilegias, lambs' ears (*Stachys lanata*) and willow make an attractive 'wild' border.*

*Lupins are known for their ability to suppress weeds and add nitrogen and phosphates to the soil; they are seen here with milk-thistle (*Silybum marianum*), an exceedingly prickly but beautiful foliage plant.*

THE SHRUB BORDER

Chapter 2 explained how we have selected and combined shrubs from woodland plants the world over and how these need to be grown with others of the same sort and background, and on sites they enjoy if they are to do well. The shrub border can be the backbone of a garden, providing a foliage and form skeleton that endures throughout the year. The permanency makes a good habitat for sheltering many forms of life and the evergreens and conifers lend themselves especially well to hiding nests and boxes. The shrubs suppress weeds fairly efficiently and rarely need watering; many are scented and most feed wildlife with berries.

My favourite scented plants are shrubs.

Daphnes are so little known and deserve much wider acclaim, though they have very poisonous berries. *D. odora* 'Aureomarginata' and *D.* x *Burkwoodii* are both beautiful and fill gardens with their scent. Viburnums mostly have excellent scent – the exceptions are the common viburnum *V. tinus* and the poisonous *V. opulus*, the Guelder rose.

Lilacs are endowed with scent only rivalled by the unsurpassable *Philadelphus*.

When you add in *Buddleia*, *Clerodendron*, *Osmanthus* and *Osmarea*, *Choisya* the Mexican orange blossom, *Santolina* the cotton lavender and the shrubby honeysuckles you hardly have room left for winter-scented shrubs.

Winter honeysuckle *Lonicera fragrantissima* has sweet little flowers powerful enough to scent rooms from November to March in mild climates, or late winter where it is colder.

Winter sweet is a *Chimonanthus* and has delicate creamy, nodding flowers, often appearing at the same time as the witchhazels (*Hamamelis*): these flower on the warmer winter days and have strong scents to attract the few insects that are about at that time of year.

Laburnum, lime, walnut and flowering cherries and almonds all have scent.

Ptelea trifoliata is an unusual little tree with a sweet scent.

Magnolia grandiflora is a very large tree and the lemon-scented flowers are the size of dinner plates.

In general shrubs and trees do well together, providing there is enough light. Climbers will choke shrubs, though. Most herbaceous plants are badly disadvantaged by shrubs but early-season, especially bulbous ones can do quite well underneath the deciduous members. Groundcover plants are detrimental to the weaker shrubs and should only be planted amongst well-established and tough-growing shrubs – as so often, *Limnanthes douglasii* is the best.

With flowering shrubs that have to be pruned, the best time is usually immediately after the flowers have faded. Always check with a specialist book before undertaking any pruning unless you are completely – and rightly – confident.

The corner of this scented shrub border finishes with my favourite plant, Daphne x burkwoodii 'Somerset Gold Edge', which is full of bloom for weeks, has a gorgeous scent and an exquisite leaf, shapely and margined in gold. The seat under the fan-trained apricot is ideally positioned for viewing the daphne.

THE MIXED BORDER

It was noted in Chapter 2 that mixing plants from different groups was not always a good idea as their needs may conflict or they may be in competition for the same resources. However, many small shrubs are commonly grown with herbaceous plants to no great detriment; bulbs and even alpines can do well. It mainly depends on each getting enough space – if this is seen to there will be far fewer problems.

This is a very mixed border with plants of differing natures and needs mixed in without careful planning – many of them are doing poorly as a result. I must get round to overhauling this soon! Pretty, though.

THE ROSE GARDEN

Roses are grown everywhere so are prone to many pests and diseases. As they are woodland plants they need moist soil with plenty of organic matter. Groundcover such as thyme, catnip and pinks helps keep the soil cool and moist. Catnip is best as it dies back, can be covered by well-rotted manure or compost and grows through again in spring. The roses can thus benefit from 'mucking', which simultaneously seals in their dead leaves with accompanying blackspot disease spores, preventing re-infection later. They benefit if underplanted with alliums, especially chives and garlic which help against blackspot, increase the perfume and deter aphids, Japanese beetles and chafers. These last two pests are also discouraged by petunias and pelargoniums. Parsley, lupins, mignonette and especially *Limnanthes douglasii* are favourable to roses. Pungent herbs help keep away pests, but box hedges are not good companions.

Roses suffer more than most plants from overpruning. Do not cut them back to a few short stubs. Remove only the sick and weak, then reduce the rest by no more than half. Leave as much growth as you can without making the plant top heavy, and you will have far more flowers over several flushes on healthier plants.

Treat climbers and ramblers in the same way with the occasional full overhaul. I prefer to weave mine like basketwork, producing masses of flowers and nest sites within. Strong ramblers romping up trees can be joined by one of the less vigorous Clematis species to increase the flowering season, as they both enjoy similar conditions. Likewise peonies can look and smell divine between standard roses.

Not the best of combinations: the mulches and soil enrichment needed for the rose may cause the iris to rot and make excessive foliage instead of flowers.

THE WATER GARDEN

Gardens developed from a protected courtyard surrounding a pool which represented an oasis to early civilization as it settled down from a nomadic existence. We carry on the association of water and gardens, perhaps recognizing the significance of water to all life – there is hardly a garden made without a watery part, be it as humble as a bird bath. Many have a pool and even the smallest patch of water can attract and sustain wildlife. It gives us more pleasure if the water is moving – a small fountain or cascade over stones adds sounds as well as visual enjoyment. (Waterlilies need still water, so separate them from moving water.)

Unless you live in a region with a cold continental climate, a pool need only be about a metre (just over three feet) deep to resist total freezing in all but the hardest winter. Stepping the sides allows for different depths and varied planting, which means that a wider range of wildlife can benefit from this habitat.

The water margin is a very important area as it supports the most forms of life. It is better to have a wide, sloping muddy edge than a neat stone slab and vertical drop. The latter may be necessary for convenience and safety, but do have at least one part where the water slowly becomes shallower and merges with a stretch of mud and plants so that animals who fall in and emergent frogs and newts can crawl out.

Provide some dense evergreens near the edge for permanent shelter and bury old pots and containers underneath as nest sites. Unless your pool is much bigger than most, try not to have overhanging trees, as the autumn leaves will sour the water; but provide a shady bit of water with taller plants such as bulrushes which are also good for birds and dragonflies to perch on. Larger areas of water can cope with some leaf debris that would overwhelm a small pool – if you have the space, willows and alder round the edge will give shelter and reinforce the banks.

Bees need access to water but drown if they fall in, so waterlilies and other plants with floating leaves help them, as do muddy edges. Butterflies similarly land on leaves or mud but birds and animals need some stepping stones – provide these as well. Birds will not bathe unless they are safe from cats, so put a stone or log in the middle of the pool for them to perch on. Do not put fish in the pool if you want newts and frogs to breed as the fish will eat the eggs.

THE OLD-FASHIONED GARDEN

A great garden is ageless, almost out of time, the illusion of an eternal summer's evening. We need a tranquil resting place to recover from the day's toil and a garden in an old-fashioned style, well blended with the surroundings, can be the perfect answer. Obviously modern materials such as plastic or asphalt should be avoided. Woodwork ought to be unplaned; it can be tarred black or creosoted brown, though the Victorians liked Eau de Nile, a sort of murky bluey green. (Creosote may be dangerous to plants and people, so handle it carefully. It is nevertheless an effective and renewable wood preservative.)

Once a traditional framework is established, traditional plants are needed to go within it. Most of our best plants were known before the turn of the century and have exceptional virtue. However many, many others equally as good have disappeared as plant production has been commercialized. There are far fewer varieties of most plants are on sale now than there were a hundred years ago, as small independent seedsmen and nurseries have been replaced by large corporations which have concentrated on the few most profitable lines. The vegetables have fared worst and the majority of those available are modern.

In the US and Canada an encouraging number of nurseries and seedsmen specializing in older varieties have sprung up in recent years, and many of them provide a mail-order service. Although it is illegal in the UK to sell seed of vegetables not on the EC-approved list, you can join private seed libraries such as that operated by the Henry Doubleday Research Association (see p. 171 for address) and acquire seed with the obligation to return some from your own crop.

You are also not allowed to plant non-approved fruit trees for commercial sale, but you may do it for your own use. There are many wonderful old apples and you can save them from likely extinction. You do not even have to have a tree of each, as you can graft many varieties on to one set of roots, each as its own branch. One friend of mine has nearly three hundred different apple varieties in one small orchard – he rarely has any pollination problems! Figs, plums, grapes and many other fruits all have varieties disappearing fast, yet almost all could be saved for other generations if they were planted in just a few gardens.

Many varieties of flowers have already gone. Where are the red-flowered lily of the valley, *Apios* the scented climber that left small cone-shaped tubers over winter, double sweet rockets, double heliotropes? It is not too late to save some of the longer-lived hardy perennials, as these still live in enthusiasts' collections. Most of the old-fashioned roses, fuchsias, pelargoniums and so on can still be found, as there are societies you can join who will help; less fashionable flowers are harder.

Mirabilis jalapa, the Marvel of Peru, is no longer seen, but is colourful and gloriously scented when the flowers open at teatime. The seed can still be found and the plants form tubers that need to be dried indoors over winter. There are many lilacs, hydrangeas, peonies and irises that are currently, undeservedly out of favour. Grow these with the old-fashioned shrub roses, the superb William Lobb, Damask, Bourbon, Moss and hybrid musks of yesteryear.

The perfect old-fashioned garden. This lovely old brick wall makes the ideal accompaniment for roses of every hue from white to deepest red.

Even if you don't want a rockery there is always a place for stone and statuary to add year-round interest: this picture was taken in my friend Will Giles' beautiful Norwich garden.

THE ROCKERY

These are out of fashion at the moment but deserve a place in naturally rocky gardens. They are an excellent way of providing wildlife shelters and of course the right conditions for alpine plants. Please exclude any rampant growers – they will just take over.

The large numbers of nooks and crannies make a rockery ideal for encouraging small predators, especially beetles but also slugs and snails, so site it away from herbaceous plants or vegetable beds. A rockery should always be situated to take advantage of any slope – if it is built on the flat it will be hard to make it blend in successfully. The classic mistake is to build a mound and dot it with rocks. Working the other way round is better, as the outermost part needs be a thick layer of rocks packed together with pockets of soil scattered about. While you are building, prepare dens for hedgehogs and other wildlife: old drums and containers can be packed with straw with tunnels of old drainpipe connecting them to the outside. Pile up the rockery on top.

It is essential to have the ground underneath weed free before you start and to use only weed-free seed and material, as weeding will be difficult later. If weeds do emerge, use a hand-held blow-torch once a week to scorch their leaves until they expire.

A loggery can be made in much the same way. Build dens and cover them over, but use old logs instead of rocks. Fill the 'pockets' with loamy, peaty compost and plant them up with woodland plants and ferns. This makes another habitat and refuge, and may even bring in woodpeckers.

THE WINTER GARDEN AND CONSERVATORY

It is surprising how many winter-flowering plants there are and how many have strong scent. In fact they need the strong scent to attract what few pollinators are about. If it is warm, bees will fly any day of the year and nectar and pollen are especially beneficial to them during the cold months when they mostly have to rely on the meagre stores we have left them with. A winter garden can be made for them, and us, in a warm corner surrounded on three sides with thick, sheltering hedges – gorse (*Ulex europaeus*) is good for this as it is evergreen and always seems to have some flowers.

Fill your corner with shrubs such as *Chimomanthus fragrans*, *Hamamelis mollis*, *Lonicera fragrantissima*, *Sarcococca*, *Mahonia japonica* and *M. bealei*, which all flower through the winter in the UK and late winter to early spring in colder climates. The early flowering bulbs such as aconites, snowdrops, crocus and dwarf iris and the tough, enchanting hellebores or Christmas roses and Lenten roses provide much early pollen for the bees. A few yellow-variegated evergreens such as *Elaeagnus pungens* 'Maculata' and *Euonymus* 'Green and Gold' add visual warmth and the pungent herbs rosemary, sage and thyme add aroma whenever anything rubs against them.

Of course you can have scented companions in comfort if you take them indoors in winter. An unheated greenhouse will protect less hardy plants through all but the worst seasons, while a heated greenhouse or conservatory allows many more tender plants to be grown for flowers and scent every day of the year.

Real lemon verbena *Lippia* or *Aloysia citriodora* has deliciously scented leaves like lemon sherbet; it is not really hardy and rarely survives long outside, but under cover it thrives and even the flowers appear and have lemon scent.

Citrus plants have lovely scents in flower, foliage and fruit and only need frost-free conditions. I have grown lemons and satsumas here in Norfolk, putting the plants out in tubs during the summer.

The scented geraniums (*Pelargonium*) and *Heliotrope* all similarly need a place indoors for the winter but can stay outside all summer. Hoyas, freesias, cyclamens, gardenias and fragrant orchids can be grown in a heated conservatory and provide some of the most exquisite scents and flowers imaginable.

THE WILD OR WOODLAND GARDEN

A wild garden needs to be as thoroughly planned as any other, and care must be taken to establish each plant well initially. Any wild area will benefit immensely from a pool and many bird and animal nest boxes.

The most useful and practical form of wild garden is the woodland edge, as this habitat provides for many interesting and attractive birds and creatures and can be enjoyable for people, too. If fruit and nut trees, brambles and berrying bushes are included, the area can also be semi-productive, though you will have to race the wildlife for every morsel.

The medlar is a strange fruit, once highly esteemed, now almost forgotten. Best left till midwinter to ripen/rot on the tree, a process called bletting, it is then traditionally eaten with cream and liqueurs.

117

Create a background and shelter belt with a dense stand of trees, shrubs and climbers; in front of this leave it to rough grass with brambles and low shrubs making screens around a 'lawn'. Cut the paths back to sward and cut either side of the paths and 'lawn' much less often, say three times a year. Under the lawn and around its perimeter, plant copious bulbs together with woodland plants such as wild strawberries, briar roses, foxgloves, lilies and Solomon's seal. Any fruit tree will be of immense benefit to wildlife and they do not grow too big for most gardens.

Some other trees are suitable. Sycamores (*Acer pseudoplatanus*) are not – they are nothing more nor less than very large weeds! These aliens help few plants or creatures and give off soil-poisoning compounds to stop other plants growing. Very little will germinate where the leaves decay. However, you should not write off the entire *Acer* genus. Sycamore is easily confused with a near relative, field maple (*A. campestre*), which is useful to wildlife.

Birch (*Betula alba*) is one of the most frost-resistant trees. In England, birch wine used to be made from the spring sap. The peeling bark impregnated with resin has insecticidal properties and is gathered for nests. Birches are the home of the classic toadstool fly agaric (*Agaricus muscarius*), once used to kill flies. Their root secretions accelerate composting, so they may be planted as screens for manure or compost bins. The soil under birches has been used to inoculate land made barren by conifers and other poisoning plants, and their presence stimulates growth in larches.

Elder (*Sambucus nigra*) is a small tree which likes rich, moist soil. The berries are a good sacrificial crop to keep birds off fruit and they make a passable jelly and an excellent wine. The leaves used to be boiled with soft soap to make an aphicide now illegal in the UK. This spray was also used against carrot root fly, cucumber beetles, peach tree borers and root maggots. Like nettles elders create a rich soil which, after clearance, leaves a fine humus. They assist composting by their presence, often seeding themselves by the bins, and are another apocryphal mole deterrent.

Oaks (*Quercus*) eventually become large trees but are slow-growing; they support more forms of life than any other tree in the temperate zone. They accumulate calcium in their bark and are beneficial to citrus groves, but in classical times were thought to hinder olives. The leaves contain much tannin and are used as mulches to protect radish and turnips, but may inhibit other plants.

Yew (*Taxus baccata*) casts heavy shade and its leaf exudations inhibit most other plants except elderberry, but its berries feed birds and the trees provide excellent nesting and hibernation sites.

Wild strawberries thrive in most situations and their flowers and fruit are valuable for the wildlife garden.

CHAPTER 6

THE PRODUCTIVE GARDEN

FOOD PLANTS AMONGST THE FLOWERS: THE MYTH OF THE COTTAGE GARDEN

Sadly, the romantic picture of the cottage garden is a gross misconception. It was never a major contributor of food. Historically, cottage gardens were full of fruit trees, herbs for medicinal use and flowers for pleasure. The bulk of the cottager's diet was beer and bread, with the addition of some field crops such as turnips and many types of wild produce. The rather kitsch cottage gardens displayed each year at the Chelsea Flower Show in London are attractive to look at but are hardly going to grow enough food for a decent meal.

A mixed border with small trees, shrubs, herbaceous plants and bulbs is difficult enough to design well and plant up effectively. It is certainly more work than devoting the same area to shrubs or herbaceous plants. To introduce food crops as well just makes for complication with very poor returns. The converse, putting 'flowers' in the productive garden, is a much better arrangement, far easier to plan and maintain. Priority is given to the productive plants: they get the best soil and situation, then the ornamentals are introduced for their companion effects and beauty. Eventually the whole garden should become – and be seen as – productive, not just with fruit and vegetables but with material for fertility and the active promotion of all forms of life.

Food crops are not often beautiful, but they can be used attractively. You can devote small beds to them as part of a formal design. These beds do not have to be rectangular; indeed, one of the most pleasing forms is the parterre or knot garden, which relies for its appeal on structure and design with a geometric pattern of small beds and paths.

Tayberries and a self-chosen companion of ox-eye daisy. The tayberry is a new, improved, loganberry-type bramble.

A plan for a geometric garden, say 11 m by 14 m (38 by 46 ft). Gravel paths about 45 cm wide are flanked with low formal hedges of Munstead Dwarf Lavender. The top bed could be planted with herbaceous plants, the bottom beds with perennial herbs and the side beds with strawberries, globe artichokes, rhubarb and annual herbs. This leaves the eight 'core' beds for the main crops of vegetables and saladings. A bird bath or other feature could decorate the central area.

This design may be more time-consuming to maintain than an allotment-style layout, but will produce sensible quantities of food attractively. It is easy to include plenty of companion plants, and the perennials can be used to create strong outlines which maintain visual interest in the winter months.

Creating a knot garden or a decorative and productive fixed-bed system makes much more sense than trying to create an idealized cottage garden with its mixture of food and flowers. Vegetables are very 'unnatural' plants – if you want high-yielding, tasty and succulent crops you have to give the plants very good growing conditions with rich soil, little competition, minimum shade and ample moisture. Does this describe the conditions in most ornamental areas of your garden?

A further complication is that if you wish to eat some of the produce you will leave a hole in the design. This greatly limits the choice of suitable plants, never mind the fact that they are unlikely to have succeeded in the first place. As for the ornamental varieties you are supposed to enjoy eating, I am sure no one who has ever tried eating an ornamental cabbage could seriously recommend it as food! Much the same goes for decorative chards, coloured maize and many herbs which most of us never eat.

It is quite easy to plan a garden to be attractive and to produce food at the same time. The main concern must be giving ample light and space to each crop. It is true that pests and disease will be less troublesome if the plants are all just mixed up, but the yields will be depressed as well. Tree or top fruits will have the best chance of all, provided they are given a good start on strong stocks so that they can grow above the other plants. Many fruiting varieties of apple, pear, peach and cherry are very ornamental in flower and are available on dwarf stocks to fit into small gardens. Fruit trees can be trained in different ways to act as screens. True quinces, *Cydonia oblonga*, not the Japanese *Chaenomeles*, are decorative in flower, leaf and form with edible fruits. Figs are attractive and can crop well. Bush fruits will probably grow reasonably well if they are provided with enough space, but most of the fruit will be lost. Draping them with nets as protection from birds does not add to the allure of a decorative area.

Redcurrants and gooseberries are easily trainable and can make decorative screens or wall coverings. Alpine strawberries are very attractive and should be used as edgings, groundcover and anywhere else. Their delicious fruit is not as readily taken by birds as that of conventional strawberries, which can be grown in most rich, moist spots: covering the fruit with jam jars will protect them against bird damage and reduce attacks of mould. Brambles and their hybrids and grapes are all easy to grow in amongst other plants, but are rather dominating and will tend to take over; as with bush fruits there is a conflict between the need to protect the fruit and the desire to make the garden look good.

Most of the herbs are more compatible with ornamental plants than the vegetables. Mint needs firm restraint or it will take over the whole area. Chives are useful and make excellent edging plants.

Saladings can be grown at the front of borders and even as ornamental parterre, knot garden or bedding plants. Unfortunately few are very

Artemisias, thymes and lavender make a sea of colour and scent.

Globe artichokes: the flower buds are a nutritious gourmet meal while the plants are among the most striking ornamentals.

decorative, they have a tendency to bolt and if you wish to eat them it leaves a gap. Salad-bowl lettuces in various colours are the most practical and relatively long lived. It is easier to have more available as food and to maintain the appearance if their replacements are continually produced in a seed bed or cold frame.

Courgettes (zucchini), marrows and ridge cucumbers can be decorative and add a tropical effect to borders but will swamp smaller plants. Their main disadvantage is that in the UK they cannot be planted out till mid-May and they get scruffy from the end of August. Sweet corn, peppers, aubergines (eggplant) and tomatoes have the same short season. Tomatoes are more practical than the others, but will require warm, sheltered positions and rich soil to produce a respectable crop.

Potatoes and root vegetables may grow, but are unlikely to be considered attractive or produce large succulent roots. Salsify and scorzonera have pretty flowers, but by the time these appear the root is old and tough. Leeks, garlic and onions also have pretty flowers which are beneficial to many insects but the flowering ruins the crop.

Peas will clamber over shrubs and look like a bad attack of bindweed; they also have a short season before they become scruffy. Runner beans and running French beans behave similarly, but the flowers of scarlet runners are very decorative and the purple-podded varieties add curiosity value. Bush beans are good companions, supplying nitrogen like all these legumes, but they are not pretty. Celery and celeriac are so demanding of rich, moist soil that it is hopeless to consider them in anything other than perfect conditions. I grow mine by the side of the pond where they do at least flourish, but rarely attain commercial proportions.

Brassicas are also very demanding and need good conditions to produce a crop. Forget any ideas you may have about growing them amongst shrubs, though they may do reasonably well in the herbaceous border. Ornamental cabbages are not very good for the table, but curly kale can make an attractive foliage plant. The mini cabbages and mini cauliflowers are more tolerant of poorer conditions and will more often give good results, but again they are nothing special to look at.

Some perennial crops are quite suitable for growing among other herbaceous plants in a border, but they take a lot of space. Globe artichokes are attractive and tasty. Cardoons look similar but are larger. Rhubarb and sea kale are other imposing foliage crop plants, while asparagus adds a delicate, feathery touch.

DIVIDING UP THE GARDEN

Because we need to give each type of crop the most suitable culture we group them according to their needs and have evolved several specialized areas in the productive garden: the fruits are split between orchard and fruit cage, vegetables are given a rich plot in full sun and the herbs often confined to one bed (though they are better spread around). Cereals and livestock are nowadays mostly confined to farms or smallholdings.

Purple Pershore plum: a luscious variety.

THE FRUIT GARDEN

Pollination is essential for almost all fruits, nuts and berries, and they need exactly the right companion as a pollinating partner. If enough pollinating agents are not available you may have problems. Early flowerers will often have finished before honey bees are about and will have to rely on bumble bees and other insects. Companion planting compensates for this by increasing the variety and seasonal availability of flowers and thus attracting more agents in greater numbers. With cherries and pears pollinating partners are nearly always critical. Some apples known as triploids are also likely to fail through lack of suitable partners.

The right partners must not only be capable of pollinating each other but must also regularly flower at the same time and be close enough for the agent to travel between them. Often the wild or a more primitive version of a cultivated tree is much the best pollinating companion. Crab apples are superb general pollinators for apples. Morello, the sour cherry, is best for most sweet cherries. Plums are an exception to this rule: it is better to pollinate them with a Victoria, which flowers in the middle of the plum season; the wild plums flower too early.

Fruit is only really good when fully mature. It ripens soonest on the sunny side of a tree or bush, so look there first. A sure sign of ripeness is damage caused by birds, wasps and other insects – they are always quicker to spot it than we are. Falling fruit usually indicates ripeness but may occur in times of drought, when a tree or bush will shed many fruit in order to preserve the rest. Unripe fruit may be accelerated to early maturity by the close proximity of dandelions, which give off ethylene gas. Bananas and ripening tomatoes will also cause quick ripening in nearby fruits, so be careful if this would be inconvenient, and store them separately. Nettles improve the ripening of fruit: grow them underneath the fruit trees or use them as hay packing in storage, where they discourage pests and diseases.

Well-intentioned but misguided pruning probably does more harm to plants than all the pests put together. Most trees and shrubs are best simply left alone. Fruit trees give more fruit earlier if they are unpruned, and shrubs and climbers will flower more profusely. We often prune just to make the plant fit the cramped space we have allowed for it. This is bad planning and it may be better to redesign rather than hack away continually at some vigorous plant in the wrong situation.

Otherwise, pruning is only necessary to establish a good initial framework, to improve flowering and/or fruiting by redirecting growth, or to cut out disease and damage. Winter pruning to remove excess growth is counter-productive as it encourages plants to grow more vigorously. Prune in winter for the first years to establish a good framework or if the tree requires major work which may shock it during the growing season. (Stone fruits like plums and cherries should never be winter pruned.) Summer pruning reduces vigour and can be used to restrict growth in favour of fruit and flowers. If plants are too big for their position, gradual summer pruning will not only allow you to see what you are leaving, but will not cause rapid replacement of the material removed.

Rochester peaches ripening on a bush in the open in my Norfolk garden.

'Doyenne du Comice' pears – as yet half grown when this photograph was taken – will be ready for eating in November. They would prefer to be on a warm wall, but at least they are sheltered.

THE ORCHARD FRUITS

We tend to put tree fruits in orchards rather than mingling them into the flower garden, partly for cultural reasons but mostly because they are simply easier to look after. Most of our fruit trees are closely related, being members of the Rosaceae family, and thus they need broadly similar conditions, though obviously each prefers slightly different treatment.

Castanea sativa Zones 5–8. Chestnuts may be more disease resistant in the vicinity of oaks. The leaves have been used to make a spray against beet moths. *C. mollissima* is the species more commonly grown in North America – the same comments apply.

Citrus spp. Not hardy in northern Europe or much of North America (yet), but easy to overwinter and move outside in pots. The flowers have exquisite scent, empty peels make good slug traps and dried are effective firelighters. Citrus trees are aided in warmer climes by rubber, oak and guava trees. They are inhibited by *Convolvulus*. Citrus fruit peel has been used for sprays against fall armyworms and bollworms.

Corylus avellana Zones 4–7. The cultivated forms of hazel such as Cosford cob or Webb's prize cob produce bigger nuts than the wild forms, yet support as many kinds of wildlife. They are beneficial in hedges and pastures for fodder and as fly deterrents. They also make excellent wind breaks.

Penstemon barbatus *is very attractive in this mixed border; growing it under apple trees is believed to discourage sawfly attacks.*

Ficus carica Zones 7–10. Figs are far hardier than most of us realize and can be grown in the open ground, though they need hot summers to ripen fruit. In zone 6 they may be grown in the open ground by wrapping the tops in winter. They do well with rue.

Juglans spp. Walnuts make very big trees that take a long time to fruit. The leaves of the American black walnut (*J. nigra*) exude chemicals that inhibit other plants, particularly potatoes, tomatoes, apples, blackberries and many ornamentals. English walnuts (*J. regia*) are less inhibiting, but do still cast heavy shade. In classical times Varro remarked on the sterility of land near walnuts, so this is an effect that has been with us for two thousand years!

Malus spp. Zones 4–9, depending on variety. Apples are grown everywhere, so they are prone to many pests and diseases. Alliums, especially chives, help protect them against scab. Sassafras oil mixed with glacial acetic acid is a bait for codling moths and can lure them away, while *Penstemon* is a pretty flower which, grown under apples, will repel their sawfly. Nasturtiums grown annually up and around the trunk of an apple tree discourage the woolly aphid.

Be careful to store only perfect fruit and to keep it away from strong herbs, potatoes and carrots. Separate late from early ripeners and use dried nettles to help preserve and ripen them. Cooking varieties benefit most from wood ashes spread underneath in early spring; dessert apples need less potash.

Apples give off ethylene gas as they ripen, which may inhibit growth and cause premature maturation in any flowers or fruits in the vicinity. The trees are believed to cause potatoes nearby to be prone to blight.

Morus nigra Zones 5–8. Mulberry trees are very slow-growing but get very big and live a long time, so be sure to plant them only where there is plenty of space. Once established they enjoy being grassed down, which also makes the fruit easier to collect. They are one of the trees over which grapevines are traditionally grown.

Prunus spp. These are all closely related and should never be pruned in winter, as this makes them prone to silver leaf disease. They prefer richer conditions than apples and their worst problem is frost killing the flowers.

P. armeniaca Zones 5 or 6–8. Apricots are surprisingly easy: try growing stones of the wild apricot Hunzas you buy from the health store for a quick, informal hedge. They may be detrimentally affected by root secretions from oats, less so by tomatoes and potatoes. Alliums, especially garlic and chives, are beneficial.

P. avium, P.cerasus These are respectively sweet cherry, zones 5–7 and sour cherry, zones 5–8. Cherries make very big trees whose surface-running roots mean they are no friends to lawns! The roots dry out the soil, which is probably why cherries suppress wheat; they may also make potatoes prone to blight.

P. persica Zones 5–8. Peaches are also easy: their main problem is that they are prone to leaf curl disease, but treating them with Bordeaux spray in spring is effective and is allowed under most organic standards. Alliums growing underneath will also help overcome the disease, as will rich mulches, equisetum and seaweed sprays. The most effective treatment is to keep the tree dry through the winter with a plastic sheet stretched over it.

P. domestica Zones 5–8. Plums benefit more than most fruit from the presence of legumes as they are very hungry consumers of minerals. Grow garlic around the base of plum trees to protect the fruit from curculios. Anemones harbour plum rust, so should not be grown nearby.

Pyrus communis Zones 5–8. A good pear is much harder to grow than a good peach. Pears need more moisture: mulches are especially useful as they keep down grass competition, which is particularly harmful to pears.

THE FRUIT CAGE

We group soft fruit together in a cage largely for economic reasons, but as it happens brambles, currants and berries are all woodland plants which like similar conditions. They have the same need for rich moist and deeply mulched root runs and most of them will tolerate light shade. Grapevines are an exception and do much better on their own – they need plenty of light and air if they are to do well. If you put them on the sunny side of a cage they will shade the others and on the dark side their fruit will not ripen successfully.

Groundcover plants can benefit soft fruit by bringing in more pollinators and predators, but be careful not to choose plants that will compete too much with the crops. The best ones are *Limnanthes douglasii* and alpine strawberries. All strong aromatic herbs can be planted outside the fruit cage or by the entrance to act as a scented barrier.

Soft fruit requires more pruning than most. Raspberries just need all the old growth cutting away after fruiting. So do blackberries and the hybrids such as loganberries and tayberries. Blackcurrants are similar, but here cut away the oldest third of the bush each year. The other currants and grapes, once established, should be summer pruned by cutting out about half of each new growth; then in winter cut it back further to a few buds.

Whitecurrant 'White Versailles', a delicious old fruit rarely grown nowadays. The juice is excellent as a lemon-juice substitute.

Fragaria spp. Strawberries are quite tender, but since they are low growing, they can be grown in fairly cold climates with a mulch and cover against snow. They have improved disease resistance if grown with onions, yet the plants may still not grow strongly. Any bean, especially French, will do well with them. Brassicas do poorly near strawberries, spinach and lettuce get on and borage will help them. They grow well at the base of peach trees and raspberries but not directly under them. They are hosts to parasites of the oriental fruit moth, which feeds on peaches, so this is another reason for growing the two together. Strawberries love mulches of pine needles. The alpine variety is a good companion anywhere, bringing in pollinators and predators all through the growing season. When establishing a new bed, grow a crop of soya beans first and dig them in green to prevent root rots on the new plants.

Ribes spp. Zones 3–6. Red and whitecurrants often suffer massive attacks of the leaf-blistering aphid, but this merely 'summer prunes' and does not affect yields. Woodland plants, they need mulching and a moist root run; they will also benefit from nettles nearby. *Limnanthes douglasii* is very good undersown as it attracts pollinators and predators, provides effective groundcover over winter and dies off when the fruit is ripening.

R. grossularia Zones 3–5. Gooseberries are much less prone to mildew when grown on a stem, although they then need staking. This allows underplanting with *Limnanthes douglasii*, which is very beneficial. Tomatoes may aid them and broad beans may drive away the sawfly caterpillar. *Veratrum*, a poisonous lily was once used to make hellebore powder for killing gooseberry sawfly caterpillars.

R. nigrum Zones 4–6. Blackcurrants are valuable high-vitamin berries which keep better if nettles are grown nearby. This also helps pest control, as predators breed up early on the aphids which nettles attract. Blackcurrants need much richer conditions than redcurrants and are not quite so prone to bird damage. In parts of the US growing blackcurrants is prohibited because they are potential hosts for white pine blister rust disease.

Rubus spp. Blackberries and their hybrids. Zones 4–8 depending on variety. A vigorous variety known as Himalayan Giant (zones 7–8) will stop a tank! Blackberries make great barriers against pests and people and are easy to grow. The bushes are sanctuaries in nature – small birds and other creatures can hide inside, protected by the arching thorns; the centres are often bone dry and provide a good place to nest or hibernate. The late flowering caters for insects in early autumn when food is becoming scarce; the fruit then feeds birds till winter.

Blackberries may aid grapevines and certainly provide a sacrificial crop at the same time as the grapes ripen. They may be aided by tansy and stinging nettles. After brambles have been cleared, the soil is often in good heart and very suitable for trees, but over-vigorous regrowth of new brambles can be a problem!

R. idaeus Zones 4–8. Raspberries are very much woodland plants needing rich, leafy, moist soil. They may encourage blight damage to potatoes, are prone to virus disease and best replaced with clean stock every ten years or so. Underplant with tansy, garlic and marigolds of any low-growing variety. Strawberries will grow in front of them but not underneath.

Vitis vinifera European grape. Zones 6–9. Grapes are exceptionally easy to grow if you choose the right variety. They need to be protected, though, or the birds will eat them. Siegerrebe (my favourite – it is superb), Schuyler and Madeleine Sylvaner will grow almost anywhere out of doors; if space can be found under cover or against a very warm wall, try Muscat Hamburgh or Chasselas d'Or. *V. vinifera* is rarely grown in the eastern US, where the American fox grape *V. labrusca*, zones 5–8, is more common – the same comments apply to this species.

Following the ancient instruction to bury a dead horse under a vine is neither easy nor hygienic and it is probably a bad idea anyway – vines should not be overfed. Growing vines over trees is a more practical tradition – elm or mulberry is best. Grapes are aided by blackberries, hyssop, sage and mustard. Legumes should be incorporated if they are put down to grass. Grapes have been thought since classical times to be inhibited by Cypress spurge, laurels, radish and cabbages. Asparagus grown underneath will not compete for light and the berries help by distracting birds.

Above: *I made my grape bower by training the vines up wires to a central pole, leaving the sunny side open to create a dappled shade that is pleasant for hot days. The grapes hang down for easy picking and there is enough light for the thornless rose on the pillar.*

Right: *Japanese wineberries are one of the best of the brambles: their delicious fruits are loved by birds and children, they are decorative with russet stems and they are bristly rather than thorny.*

This wonderful thornless rose 'Zéphirine drouhin' graces the entrance to my vegetable garden of forty raised beds, each 1.2 x 5 m (4 x 16 ft).

THE VEGETABLE GARDEN

Flowers make me humble but vegetables make me proud

The vegetables are a very mixed bunch. For centuries we have grown them together purely for our convenience, with little thought to their differing origins. As a result many mismatches, bad companions and inferior varieties have had to be eliminated over the years to give us the crops we grow today.

Strangely, considering the care many people exercise over the cultivation of vegetables, we generally seem to be more concerned with annual rotations than with any interactions the plants might have while they are actually growing together! We grow them well spaced out in rich soil without shade or weeds just so that they can produce specimens of the size and quality we expect – and then all too many gardeners ignore the effects of the plants that are put right next to them.

Vegetables are not just important food crops, they are highly bred and they are all being asked to perform far better than they ever would in the wild. So anything we can do to help will give them more chance of producing the 'unnatural' yields we require. In the UK it is common practice to plant vegetables in long, thin rows one plant across. This means that each plant is flanked by two different sets of plants, along the whole length of the row, and the plants are rotated every year. Regrouping plants so that they aid rather than detract from one other is an obvious thing for the companion gardener to consider.

128

Raised beds, fixed beds and rows

Raised beds are an easy way to make life difficult. Too many novices go for these straight away without first mastering gardening on the flat with fixed beds. The main reasons to use either are to allow no-digging methods, with block planting in preference to row planting, and to make rotation easier. Fixed beds give most of the advantages of raised beds, are easier to manage and after a few years they become raised beds anyway: pathways are trodden down and the beds slowly rise as material is added and the texture improves. If the paths are cleared regularly, the scrapings placed on top of the beds soon help build up more height. Raised beds have better microclimates and the higher working level saves the worst of the bending.

Raised beds are one of the better ways of managing the soil, giving an increased surface area which promotes aeration and warms the soil very quickly in the spring. Cold air runs off the beds, keeping the top slightly more frost free, and crops winter better as waterlogging is unlikely.

On the down side, raised beds continue to dry out quickly throughout the year, so they require more watering before sowing or transplanting. Light rain penetrates, but heavy rain may just run off and be lost. Mulches slide or are kicked off by birds, so pathways have to be cleared regularly.

Align raised or fixed beds north-south to prevent excessive shading. A size of about 1.2 m (4 ft) by 5 m (16 ft) is ideal – any wider and the middle is hard to reach; any longer and beds are inevitably trodden on as they are used as a short cut.

Raised beds with rigid sides are expensive to set up in terms of both time and materials and the planks used to form the sides provide too many hidden shelters for pests as well as for friendly creatures. Mounding the soil with slopes on all sides maximizes the growing area and does away with the need for rigid sides. The varying slopes and aspects of parts of a raised bed all have their own microclimates and can be used for different crops or to spread the cropping season. In the northern hemisphere, the hot, sunny south end will always crop ahead of the cool, moist, north-facing end; the sides will be cooler, more sheltered and moister than the top, but not as shady as the north end.

The two ends are ideally suited for growing companion border plants: put the Mediterranean herbs at the hot south end and the moisture-loving ones on the shady north slope. This leaves the bulk of the bed for the main planting and brings the companions into close proximity. Planting within each bed can still be in rows, but for many crops block planting will prove to be better.

Whether you choose raised or fixed beds, you will save yourself work compared with row planting. The paths of either a raised or a fixed bed are permanent; because the beds are are not walked on, the soil doesn't become compacted and they therefore only need digging every seven years or so. With row culture the paths are all impermanent and are quickly compacted, which means the whole area has to be dug every year. Rows should be aligned north-south, as above, and again they should not be made too long for convenience. More space is lost to plants with row culture, and more plants are unavoidably brushed against while we are working in the garden. This greatly increases the risk of diseases attacking the damaged surfaces, and the scent released may attract and guide pests.

Dividing the vegetable garden up into fixed beds, whether raised or not, has one great advantage and that is the creation of more manageable units. Rather than weeding the whole area, it is easier to concentrate on the most critical beds, leaving the others till later. Planning and allocating what goes where becomes easier – beds can be devoted to one crop with a few beneficial companions or filled with mixtures of plants that go well together. Whatever style of planting you choose, it is always advisable to keep some records so that crops can be rotated effectively.

Rotation

Rotation is vitally important. Each year in any given bed a crop extracts different requirements from the soil and leaves different residues for the next. Those that root deeply and those that are shallow exploit all the layers over three or four years and keep the soil more active throughout.

The important thing to remember is that the benefit comes from rotation itself, not from sticking to a specific scheme. Almost any rotation will be of benefit and it is by no means essential to follow those neat charts to be found in most books. It is particularly difficult to follow someone else's plan if you do not want exactly the same proportions of different crops; factors such as variation in soil add to the complications.

Rotation is more important for some crops than for others because they are commonly grown and thus there are many pests and diseases waiting to attack in every locality. Hungry feeders such as the brassicas, sweet corn, potatoes and tomatoes need to be alternated with light feeders such as onions, roots, peas and beans, but generally speaking change for change's sake alone is a good thing.

Rotation controls pests and diseases by removing the susceptible crop from their immediate vicinity before they have the chance to build up over several generations. Larvae and spores left in the soil after any crop has been cleared emerge to find a less susceptible plant – or a totally unsusceptible one – in the same place the following year. The cultural conditions required for each crop and the microclimate it produces vary, so weeds are continually disadvantaged and prevented from building up. The weeds that flourish in amongst the peas, for example, are not going to like the harsh, windswept openness under sweet corn.

The first crops to consider in any rotation are the brassicas. We grow so many types and varieties of these that we often want more of them than will fit into the usual scheme for a three- or four-year rotation. They come best after the peas and beans, which leave nitrogen for them. They also need lime, which will aid the legumes, too. Lime is best applied with the peas or beans and will remain active in the soil for the following brassica crop, but must have time to incorporate before the potatoes arrive – they get scab if exposed to too much of it.

With beds it is possible to squeeze in more of the same crops than with rows, as you can rotate crops within each bed as well as from bed to bed. For example, a row of cauliflowers can be planted along the middle of a bed where a row of peas grew previously. Blocks of onions can go on

Brassicas are useful after we have finished with them: bees and early butterflies adore the flowers.

either side, where sweet corn was earlier flanking the peas. The next year a root crop might cover the whole bed and the year after that brassicas can be planted again, but this time along the flanks where the onions were. As it is only two years since the cauliflowers were in the same bed, although not in the same place, the advantage gained is slight. It is greatly increased if widely differing brassicas are alternated rather than closely related ones. Do not follow cauliflowers with cauliflowers or broccoli but with Brussels sprouts or cabbages, then perhaps kale the next time, and so on. Kohlrabi, turnips, swedes, Chinese cabbage and radishes are more distantly related to the other, more cabbage-like brassicas, so can be happily alternated with them, incurring even less risk of building up pest and disease problems.

To give time for the lime to be incorporated before potatoes are grown, the brassicas are usually followed by a root crop such as carrots or parsnips. These do not like soil with lumps of compost or manure in it, as this causes forked roots, and they will not mind the lowered fertility left by the brassicas.

Well-rotted manure and compost will suit the potatoes, though, and will offset any lime still free in the soil. Applied at the same time as the potato sets are sown, it will leave plentiful humus for sweet corn or marrows, squashes and other hungry feeders. Tomatoes are closely related to potatoes, so keep them as far apart in the rotation as possible. They can fill the fourth slot (after peas or beans, brassicas and roots) in alternate four-year cycles and occupy different positions. Potatoes are usually best suited to the flanks of a bed, while tomatoes appreciate the more open conditions on top.

Beyond the shallots in the foreground are three beds of peas and potatoes. The hardier peas down the middle are flanked by potatoes and these are later interplanted with sweet corn. All the crops compete, but the total yield of all three crops from these three beds is higher than if there is just one bed of each.

Sweet corn is best grown in a block, so I grow it on three raised beds giving one enormous block. The plants let plenty of light through, so I run rows of peas down the middle of each bed with the sweet corn on either side and potatoes planted to spill over on to the paths.

Catch and intercropping

Catch cropping means raising an extra, quick-growing crop in a piece of ground before the main crop is ready to be planted or needs all the space to itself. It is easier to catch crop if plants are started off in seed-beds or better still in multi-celled packs. Then the catch and main crop plants can be grown under cover and planted out as small plants with their roots undisturbed. Starting small numbers of plants like lettuce and beetroot in a pack every week or so means that whenever a space becomes available you have some plants ready to fill it.

Intercropping is really just another name for companion planting – crops that get on well and don't compete for the same resources are grown together.

Pollination

Vegetable crops rarely suffer from pollination problems – most do not need it and those that do have no trouble provided sufficient agents have been encouraged. Runner beans may need helping with water sprayed on their flowers. Indoor tomatoes, peppers and the marrows and courgettes (zucchini) benefit from hand pollination early in the year when the greenhouse is tightly closed. Sweet corn should be planted in blocks as it is wind pollinated. Take particular care with some of the new, extra sweet varieties: they must not be grown with other varieties, as they do not succeed if they are cross-pollinated.

Shallots drying on a rack so that they will store well. Keep them away from apples or pears or they may taint.

Harvest and storage

Old freezers make excellent insulated root stores and are much easier to find space for than traditional root cellars or clamps. Lift the roots, from dry soil if possible; store only the perfect vegetables, using up any damaged ones first. Twist off the leaves, as cutting them will cause bleeding. Do not wash the plants, but gently brush off excess soil and store them in layers of ever so slightly moist peat, sand or sawdust. Examine them regularly and remove any rot.

Potatoes are best kept separately from other roots and fruits. They need to be cool but frost free and out of any light. They must be dug in dry conditions and only the best saved in paper sacks – again, a dead freezer makes an excellent storage place.

Onions, shallots and garlic should be lifted in dry weather and allowed to dry in a warm spot for as long as possible, then kept frost free in airy conditions. Hanging them in bunches or net bags from the roof of the potting shed is the traditional thing to do, but the garage may serve as well.

Vegetables in the greenhouse or under cover

Economic necessity often forces all the tender plants to share the same greenhouse and it is hardly surprising that some fail to thrive: tomatoes need warm, dry conditions and cucumbers need warm, moist ones, so they cannot be expected to do well together. It is a good idea to divide up a greenhouse internally so that you can provide different plants with the conditions they need. A cold frame in the greenhouse will give a superbly warm and protected environment, but there will then be problems with poor light. To counteract this, glass should always be kept clean and electric growing lights are useful on dark days.

Watering and ventilation are critical, and automatic systems are really essential to prevent growth ever being checked. The need to keep the warmth in during cold springs means that early-flowering crops will need hand pollination, as natural agents can't gain access. Later on the pollinators can be encouraged into the greenhouse with good companions such as marigolds and sweet alyssum, which I find particularly effective. Bumble bees can now be bought commercially in cardboard nests, so this is one way of improving pollination early in the season.

Pest control under cover is particularly difficult as the natural checks and balances cannot take place. The use of companions will help immensely – in ten years I have never had whitefly in my greenhouse as I grow *Tagetes* marigolds, basil and tomatoes together. Beetles and toads can be encouraged with rubble nests in a shady corner and groundcover or green manure plants covering the soil.

Vegetables can be divided up into groups within which the individual members have much in common or are very closely related, and so have very similar likes, dislikes and cultural requirements: alliums, brassicas, cucurbits, Solanaceae, legumes, other seed crops, leaf crops and roots.

Alliums

The onion genus is related to the lilies and all the species have a strong smell which can help hide other plants from pests. They accumulate sulphur, producing a fungicidal effect. Chives are often grown under roses for this purpose and hide the lower stems into the bargain. Garlic is said to improve the roses' perfume and both discourage aphids. Reputed to repel moles (you should be so lucky), they are among the most effective companions for many plants, but *not* for the beans. If left to flower they are much loved by bees and other insects.

Allium cepa Onions and beans mutually detest each other, peas do not get on well with onions, but the brassicas do. Beets, tomatoes and lettuce grow well with them and benefit from the association, as it helps protect them from slugs and snails. The same applies to onions and strawberries. This last, strange-looking combination always raises an eyebrow, but the onions will grow well and prevent moulds on the strawberries, though the growth of the strawberry plants is inhibited.

Summer savory may be beneficial to onions, though it also helps beans. Small amounts of chamomile are also helpful. Carrots are often intercropped so that the onion and carrot flies are muddled by the smells: adding leeks as well increases the confusion. Onions may deter Colorado beetles.

When the onions are swelling and ripening it is beneficial to let the weeds grow, as this takes up spare moisture and nutrients, particularly nitrogen, and the bulbs then keep better.

PERENNIAL HERBS

These may benefit the vegetables but are too difficult to grow *with* them. Instead they can be planted as borders and edging to the plot: Catnip, chamomile, chives, comfrey, deadnettle, horseradish, hyssop, lemon balm, lovage, marjoram, rosemary, sage, southernwood, tansy, tarragon, thyme, valerian, yarrow. Great care should be taken with horseradish and comfrey as they are difficult to eradicate. For more details of benefits offered by specific herbs, see pp. 144–147.

These potatoes and onions did not do well together – the onions alone on the next bed fared much better.

All alliums have fungicidal properties and attract beneficial insects; these A. sphaerocephalum *are a case in point.*

A. porrum Leeks are not as destructive to beans as other alliums and like to be with onions, celery or carrots. They will decrease attacks of carrot root flies and hide brassicas from pigeons, but may not get on well with broccoli. Nettles and nettle sprays will protect them from leek fly and leek moth.

A. sativum Garlic is the most pungent of the alliums and an effective accumulator of sulphur, which may explain its ancient reputation as a fungicide. Garlic emulsion kills aphids and onion flies; it has also been used against codling moths, snails, root maggots, Japanese beetles, carrot root fly and peach leaf curl. Putting cloves of garlic in with grain will discourage weevils.

Plant cloves in the autumn for bigger yields, but do not put them in too deep. Garlic is not as attractive as chives for planting as a companion, though is especially good for roses and fruit trees and mutually beneficial with vetch. Keep garlic away from beans or peas, though they may follow in rotation.

Brassicas

The members of the cabbage genus are all highly bred and very specialized, so they need rich soil and plenty of lime. They benefit from the presence of herbs such as chamomile, dill, peppermint, rosemary and sage, which help repel pests, especially the cabbage white butterfly. Cannabis plants used to be popular with Dutch growers as borders to brassicas for the same reasons, but growing them is now illegal in most countries.

Brassicas do well with peas, celery, potatoes, onions and dwarf beans, but not with rue, lettuce or strawberries. Most of them are unhappy with runner beans, though Brussels sprouts are more tolerant than the rest. French beans will reduce damage from root fly and mealy aphis. Cabbage root flies are found dead in great numbers on the underside of the leaves of cucurbits, especially pumpkins. This may be coincidence, though, as examination shows that they die of an entomophagous fungus attack.

Tomatoes are controversial: they *may* aid

VEGETABLE GROUPINGS

Rather than try to remember all the idiosyncrasies of each crop, group them together with those that have similar needs. Some can readily be grown from home-saved seed and others are easily propagated vegetatively – both these operations save expenditure on new plants. Many are best sown *in situ*, while others are easier to start in a seed-bed or under cover.

Crops you can grow easily from your own seed include: alpine strawberries, asparagus, asparagus peas, beans, beetroot, carrots, cucumbers, leeks, marrows, melons, onions, parsnips, peas, pumpkins, salsify, spinach, tomatoes, turnips, watermelons.

Plants that can be easily grown from offsets, tubers or cuttings include: blackberries, chives, currants, figs, globe artichokes, gooseberries, grapes, horseradish, Jerusalem artichokes, leeks, potatoes, raspberries, rhubarb, runner beans (overwinter the roots like dahlias), sea kale, shallots, strawberries, tree onions.

Plants best sown direct where they are to grow: beans, carrots, chicory, Chinese cabbage, Hamburg parsley, Japanese or autumn onions, parsnips, peas, radishes, salsify, scorzonera, spring onions, swedes, turnips.

Plants best sown in a seed-bed (preferably transplanted once to form better rootballs) for planting out: Brussels sprouts, broccoli, cabbages, cauliflowers, kale, leeks.

Plants that can conveniently be sown under cover in multi-celled packs or small pots: beetroot, chards, most herbs, kohlrabi, lettuce and saladings, onions, parsley, spinach.

Plants best started under cover in bigger pots: globe artichokes, sweet corn, extra early peas and beans, ridge cucumbers and gherkins, marrows, squashes and pumpkins. Celery and celeriac do better with heat.

Plants that need heat to germinate early enough to produce a successful crop: basil, courgettes (zucchini), cucumbers, hot peppers, melons, okra, sweet peppers, tomatoes, watermelons.

spring cabbage (though I think this is unlikely as the seasons hardly touch). They do attract the cabbage butterflies from the brassicas and deter flea beetles, but they hinder broccoli and are themselves severely inhibited by its presence. Perhaps it is best to avoid growing tomatoes and brassicas near each other: instead, try using pieces of tomato to deter flea beetles from the brassicas.

Brassicas are prone to clubroot disease, so if you do not have it in your garden, *never* introduce brassica plants from anywhere else, however short of them you may be. It is better to do without, as once present this disease is almost incurable. Some small protection has been found from incorporating garlic or rhubarb pieces or extracts in the planting holes. A green manure crop of ryegrass dug in before the brassicas will also help reduce damage from clubroot.

B. oleracea Acephala Group
Kale is a typical brassica but tougher than most and very hardy; it will survive most winters.

B. o. Gemmifera Group
Brussels sprouts have most of the general Brassica tendencies, differing mainly in that they have more tolerance for runner beans and a liking for really firm soil. They may be bad for grapevines.

B. o. Botrytis Group
Cauliflowers are cauliflowers in the warm months, but the winter ones are botanically broccolis. They are the most highly bred of the brassicas and the most difficult to grow well because the part we eat is an enormous, multiple-flowered head suspended in the bud stage and any check or damage will lead to 'button' heads.

Cauliflowers have much the same companionships as the other brassicas, strongly disliking tomatoes and strawberries. Celery may help keep away white butterfly. It is said that cauliflowers will never do well in a bed where they follow spinach.

B. o. Capitata Group
Cabbages are immensely swollen terminal buds. They can be aided and protected by strong herbs. Grow dill, mints, rosemary, sage, thyme, hyssop and chamomile nearby. Avoid strawberries. Cabbages may also not get on with grapes. One old companion idea was to plant wormwood or southernwood with them to drive away the white butterflies. It works, but the leaf exudations poison them, lowering yields significantly. Similarly, tomatoes are often recommended as companions to keep flea beetles off cabbages, but they are not very effective at this and do badly themselves. Summer cabbages can be protected from mealy aphis and whitefly attacks by surrounding them with French beans sown three weeks after the cabbages.

B. o. Gongylodes Group
Kohlrabi is a tough and disease-resistant crop much like a turnip but easier to grow, less vulnerable to drought and not as hot to the taste. It does not get on with tomatoes, strawberries, peppers or runner beans, but does with onions, beet and cucumber.

B. rapa Pekinensis Group
Chinese cabbage, Pe Tsai, needs almost boggy conditions and sowing after midsummer to succeed. It grows well with Brussels sprouts. Eaten by flea beetles, slugs and aphids, it makes a useful sacrificial or trap crop once the inevitable bolting sets in. In the US it can be used as a sacrifice to maize crops as it attracts their cornworms.

B. rapa Rapifera Group
Turnips are normally thought of as root vegetables, but are actually brassicas, with many of their traits. They get on well with peas, are aided by hairy tare (*Vicia hirsuta*), which keeps off aphids, and do not like hedge mustard or knotweeds.

Cucurbitaceae
These are all very similar, needing warm, moist conditions and a rich soil to do well. They are normally grown under cover, so may require pollinating, and are prone to neck rot: grow them on top of little mounds to prevent this. Although they must have warmth, they often do best in dappled shade.

Citrullus lanatus
Watermelons like groundcover as they prefer the shade and moist conditions this offers, but only if the sun is already hot enough for them. Potatoes provide a useful combination of shelter and dappled shade. Like melons (see next entry), watermelons need heat and are very susceptible to red spider mite.

Cucumis melo
Melons need warm, very moist, rich conditions. Morning glory (*Ipomoea*) is said to stimulate germination of the seeds, though this may have been confused with Convolvulus. Melons like sweet corn, peanuts and sunflowers, but not potatoes. They accumulate calcium in their leaves and are very prone to red spider mite – moist conditions discourage this pest.

Cucumis sativus
Cucumbers need rich, moist, warm conditions. The plants are self-pollinating; cross-pollination produces bitter fruits on indoor varieties, so male flowers should be removed. Outdoor or ridge cucumbers do not become bitter; they do well in the light shade under maize or sunflowers, so these can be grown as natural canes to train the cucumbers up.

They like peas and beans, beets, radishes and carrots but dislike potatoes (the feeling is mutual) and most strong herbs, especially sage. Dill may aid the plants (and goes well with them pickled) and will make a trio with sweet corn. Nettle tea helps prevent cucumbers succumbing to attacks of downy mildew. Tansy plants and radishes discourage cucumber beetles. Cucumbers may be used as a sacrificial crop to lure whitefly away from tomatoes.

Cucurbita pepo
Pumpkins, marrows and squashes need rich soil and copious water if they are to grow really big. They may be healthier in the presence of *Datura* weeds; they dislike potatoes and do well under sweet corn. Courgettes (zucchini) are the same plants as marrow, bred to produce lots of little fruits. Grow them with sweet corn, peas and beans and avoid potatoes.

Solanaceae
Most of this family are grown under cover in the UK. In hot climates they are staples in the summer garden. Tomatoes will grow outdoors in warmer areas, but are more reliable inside. Potatoes are the exception and do well outside. These plants are prone to the same pests and diseases and all prefer rich, moist soil.

Capsicum annuum
Sweet or bell peppers are vulnerable to aphids and like basil, which grows well with them. Avoid kohlrabi.

C. frutescens
Hot chilli peppers are also prone to aphids, but the ground, dried fruit and seeds are effective at discouraging many pests. Some chillis have root exudates that inhibit *Fusarium* diseases.

Lycopersicon esculentum
Tomatoes are so closely related to potatoes that the two crops should be kept apart. Like most plants they loathe fennel and wormwood; they also dislike all the brassicas, especially kohlrabi. They may aid early cabbage – though this seems unlikely as their growing seasons do not really overlap. However, bits of the leaf do repel flea beetles. Tomatoes get on well with basil, alliums, marigolds and nasturtiums. They keep for longer if grown near nettles. Some varieties agree, some disagree with parsley, or so it would seem. Tomatoes do particularly well with asparagus. Tomato leaf spray has been used against asparagus beetles and the asparagus roots kill *Trichodorus*, a nematode that attacks tomatoes.

Dandelions exude cichoric acid, which protects tomatoes from *Fusarium* wilt disease. A strange but effective combination is tomatoes protecting roses from blackspot. Tomatoes may also inhibit apricot seedlings and may be protective to gooseberries. Biodynamic growers put them in the same place year after year without rotation and feed them compost made from their own leaves. Interestingly, they have been shown to take up antibiotics from the soil.

Solanum tuberosum
Potatoes are highly bred and very commonly grown, so they are more than usually vulnerable to pests and diseases – keep them well away from tomatoes (which do not get on with cabbages, though potatoes do). Horseradish is often planted to aid potatoes in Europe and in China; it destroys eelworms, but is very vigorous, so must be carefully contained. Peas are of considerable benefit to potatoes. *Tagetes* marigolds are helpful, as are celery, flax, cannabis, lamiums,

nasturtiums and summer savory. Potatoes are mutually beneficial with beans and maize. Sunflowers, cucurbits, orache, many trees and raspberries are not good for potatoes, however.

In the US aubergine (eggplant) can be used as a sacrificial crop to lure the Colorado beetle away from potatoes. Potato eelworm is harboured by black and woody nightshade, so these should be weeded out as soon as they are spurred into germination by potatoes. *Tagetes* will kill many of the eelworms, as will a green manure of mustard, barley or oats grown beforehand. Onions and other alliums going before will prevent *Rhizoctonia* infections. Scab can be avoided by putting grass clippings and comfrey leaves in with the sets. Potatoes are easily spoiled or tainted in store, so keep them away from strong odours and ripening or rotting fruits.

Phytophora infestans or potato blight is a common problem which also affects tomatoes. Worst in warm, wet summers, it is overwintered on tubers which form new plants on the old site and may harbour a variety of pests and diseases. Spacing, effective earthing up and removal of haulm once an infection starts will produce a crop most years; growing early varieties gives lower yields that come before the blight starts. Many trees, raspberries, sunflowers, and cucurbits may make potatoes more prone to this disease. Growing *Cannabis sativa* may deter blight, but will encourage interest in your horticultural endeavours from the local constabulary or police department. Allium, nettle, equisetum and seaweed sprays may offer some protection.

S. melongena Aubergine (eggplant) is often grown with peppers, even though they are related, as both crops like the same warm, rich conditions. Aubergines also grow well with peas, tarragon and thyme and can be protected from Colorado beetles by interplanting with beans.

Legumes
Although we eat the immature pods of some members of the family, legumes are mostly grown for the seeds which the plants are by their very design striving to produce. They are therefore easy crops to grow, as we are not pushing the plants against their nature. They have the ability to fix nitrogen from the air with the aid of

bacteria living in nodules on their roots. If the soil has never grown legumes before, inoculating it with these bacteria (which are available commercially) before planting will help. Once the plants die, the roots decay and the nitrogen becomes available to other plants.

In general legumes detest the alliums and gladioli, but do well with carrots and beets and help cucumbers. They may be grown with borage, potatoes, squashes, strawberries and tomatoes. They are very beneficial to brassicas, protecting them from mealy aphis and root fly attacks. They may aid leeks, but only when present in a small proportion; the same is true of celeriac. Legumes are also good with sweet corn and cereals.

In the US marigolds will protect beans against the Mexican bean beetle, as will petunias, potatoes, rosemary and summer savory. Potatoes in return will be protected from the Colorado beetle, but more importantly the beans produce a root exudation which kills wireworms so can be used to clear up infestations or to protect potato and root crops from them. When sowing beans, dip them in salad oil and they will be less prone to mould.

These runner beans can ramble over the same support as the squashes and will not choke them if grown for a late crop.

Glycine max
Soya beans are too tender for most European gardeners. They are hosts to *Trichogramma* wasps and have been used to deter cinchworms, chinch bugs, corn earworms, corn borers and Japanese beetles. Dug in as a green manure before strawberries are planted, they prevent attacks of root rots.

Phaseolus coccineus
Runner beans are inhibited by onions and dislike kohlrabi and sunflowers – which is a shame, as they grow well with and up sweet corn, which likes sunflowers. When grown over maize they protect it from corn armyworms. They get on with most brassicas, especially Brussels sprouts, which are sheltered while small and then grow on once the beans die back, flourishing on the nitrogen these leave. They can be a problem late in the season, when they tend to shade out other crops. This may benefit some, especially celery and saladings, but only when enough water is available.

Runner beans are perennial and can be protected or overwintered like dahlias for an earlier crop. Yields can be improved by growing them with sweet peas to bring in pollinators.

P. vulgaris
French or dwarf beans are also known as waxpod, snap, string or green beans; there is even a running French bean. They do well with celery when planted in rich, moist soil and produce earlier crops with strawberries, which also benefit. They are very helpful to summer cabbages, which should be sown three weeks before the beans to get the best pest protection from them. Tomatoes will reduce the damage to beans caused by leaf hoppers.

Pisum sativum
Peas go well with the roots and beans, celeriac, cucurbits or sweet corn, and I find them good with potatoes. They get on with most herbs, but only in situations where they do not cast too much shade. Peas do not like many of the alliums, though they will tolerate leeks. Gladioli are supposed not to like peas, but I have had no problem with sweet peas. Root exudates from peas increase the availability of nitrogen, phosphorus, potassium and calcium.

Two rows of broad beans support and shelter a row of sweet peas for cutting; bees love the leek heads seen flowering on a nearer bed.

Vicia faba
Broad beans are winter hardy from zone 8 south and are often sown in autumn to avoid the black aphid; this may be discouraged by summer savory, which also cooks well with beans. Nipping out the bean tips above the flowers is a more effective aphid control. Spinach will benefit from the shade of the beans and in return will help discourage black fly attacks. Broad beans are a good crop to grow before maize, as they leave a rich, moist soil and the stubs can give wind protection to the young shoots.

Field crops of beans smell sweet and provide a lot of nectar for bees; the haulm makes a good base for bedding and sheet composts. Mutually beneficial with potatoes, both can be sown in the autumn for earlier crops if the winter is mild. The seedling beans protect the early spring potato shoots from wind and frost. Planted with gooseberries they discourage sawfly caterpillars.

Other seed crops
Although these are not leguminous they are easy to grow, as again we are encouraging the plant to do what nature intended anyway.

Helianthus annuus
Sunflowers are good for bees, lacewings and predatory wasps. The seeds are much loved by wild birds and hens, as well as for human snacks. Hungry feeders, sunflowers inhibit many plants, especially potatoes, runner beans and grass, and grass in turn inhibits their germination. They get on with sweet corn and the two are mutually protective: the sunflowers also act as windbreaks. Cucumbers and other cucurbits grow well underneath given enough richness and water.

Sweet corn (Zea mays) and squashes do very well together: this combination was used by native Americans a thousand or more years ago.

Zea mays

Sweet corn, not to be confused with what is called maize in Europe – that is a variety grown for animal fodder and not good for human consumption. This crop was traditionally grown in hillocks covering a dead fish. Incorporating fishmeal, seaweed meal or compost is the modern alternative, as corn needs rich soil. It should follow a legume or grow with one. It does well with all beans and the Basques grow runner beans up and over the corn. It does particularly well with peas, which then crop for longer. The light shade corn provides makes it friendly to cucumbers, melons, squashes, courgettes (zucchini), marrows and even potatoes.

Tomatoes and corn are fine together in Europe, but in the US may aid the earworm common to both. On the other hand, corn does repel cucumber beetles. Intercropping it with sunflowers increases yields of both. Brussels sprouts do best of all the brassicas with corn, though kale, savoys and broccoli can also be interplanted. When the corn is cleared in early autumn it allows them a final spurt of growth before winter.

Leaf and shoot crops

These are the easiest crops to grow badly. By their nature they will produce the parts we eat, but if we wish these to be soft and succulent the plants will generally require very rich, moist conditions. Any check and most of them will bolt.

Amaranthus retroflexus

Amaranth is only infrequently grown in Europe but is a highly nutritious tropical annual which can be used like spinach in a salad. It is beneficial to sweet corn and onions and its shade encourages ground beetles.

Asparagus officinalis

Zones 4–8. Asparagus is traditionally grown in French vineyards as it likes the conditions under grapes and the berries fob off the birds. It does well with tomatoes, which will protect it from the asparagus beetle. A root secretion from asparagus kills *Trichodorus*, a nematode that attacks tomato roots. Asparagus and tomatoes both like basil and the three do extremely well together. Parsley also does well with asparagus, but only if it can get the moisture on which it thrives. Asparagus dislikes onions and possibly other alliums as well.

Atriplex hortensis, *A. hastata* in the US. Orache is an unusual, spinach-like vegetable which grows tall. It is thought to inhibit potatoes, especially if it is given the chance to overtop them.

Lactuca sativa

Lettuces are best sown little and often as catch and intercrops. They thrive among cucumbers, parsnips, carrots, radishes and strawberries, but may not prosper near broccoli. Chervil can protect them from aphids and slugs. If it is hot, sow lettuces in the shade, as they will not germinate at temperatures above about 18°C (65°F). Lettuce is one of the plants that has been shown to take up natural antibiotics from the soil.

Rheum rhaponticum Zones 3–8. Rhubarb is a traditional aphicide – the boiled leaves contain the poison oxalic acid. The same spray has been used against blackspot on roses. The plant may help deter red spider mites from aquilegias. It is reputed to control clubroot and root flies in brassicas if included in the sowing or planting hole, but sadly tests have rarely shown that it brings any great benefit.

Spinacia oleracea

Spinach grows well near strawberries and is superb as a short-term green manure, of benefit to almost all crops except cauliflower. It should be much more widely used, as it is so easily incorporated back into the soil and aids humus formation, being rich in saponins which bind together soil particles and give it a good structure. Spinach may be mutually suppressive with radishes, especially when either is bolting. For the best results of all, plant spinach in a rotation following broad beans.

Root crops

These are mostly biennial, growing fat roots one year to flower the next. They are therefore hard to grow well, as any check or hindrance causes them to bolt. Although they need rich, moist soil, do not overfeed them or use fresh manure, as either will cause poor flavour and forked roots.

Apium graveolens
Celery is a hard crop to grow well, as it must never dry out, is prone to bolting and suffers from slug damage. It needs to be blanched, with light being excluded with cardboard wrappings and earthing up. Self-blanching types are hardly so and are tougher textured. Celery does well with beans and tomatoes, benefits brassicas by deterring cabbage white butterflies, but grows best of all with leeks. If left to flower, celery and leeks will attract many beneficial insects, especially predatory wasps. Celery rust can be prevented with tea made from nettles and equisetum. Celery seed is also good in baking.

A. g. rapaceum
Celeriac is easier to grow than celery, but still needs constant moisture. Remove the lowest leaves and any surface roots to make the crown swell. It grows best in rich soil following legumes, especially after a green manure of vetch, and also does well between rows of runner beans if kept moist – spraying helps the bean flowers set. A good companion to grow with leeks, which can be tolerated by runner beans but only make a trio where moisture is abundant. Celeriac will do well with most brassicas, onions and tomatoes. Nettle teas will help keep off celery fly and leaf spot.

Beta vulgaris
Beets. Many associated plants make up this genus: red, yellow and sugar beet are very closely related to leaf beet, perpetual spinach and Swiss chard. Originating from maritime regions, they need trace elements more than most crops (see p. 157). They thrive on seaweed products but do poorly in impoverished, chemically fertilized soil. Good mineral accumulators, one quarter of the mineral content of their leaves is magnesium, which is extremely valuable when added to the compost.

Beets do well growing with most beans, though not with the runners. They like lettuce, onions and brassicas, especially kohlrabi. However, the brassica-related weeds charlock and wild mustard are particularly detrimental. If beets follow an onion crop they are less likely to suffer eelworm attacks. They prevent corncockle seeds from germinating. If any of the beets start to bolt and form flower stems, they should be pulled to stop them encouraging

others. The most troublesome pests are birds eating the seeds, seedlings and young leaves: I hide beets among other less vulnerable crops such as turnips and swedes.

Daucus carota
Carrots are plagued by their root fly, but numerous herbs and strong-smelling remedies, especially onions, leeks and salsify, have been used against them with some success. Rosemary, wormwood and sage help confuse the pest with their scents, but the best preventative is crop rotation and a physical barrier of old net curtain to stop the fly laying its eggs on the seedling carrots. Their health is better near chives, celery, lettuce, radishes and tomatoes. They promote growth in peas but dislike anise and dill, although the latter discourages the root fly.

Before sowing carrots, improve heavy soil with a green manuring of flax and in the US of soya beans (which will not prosper in the UK). Carrots do well if they follow onions, and if left to flower they attract hoverflies and wasps. Carrots stored near apples may acquire a bitter taint.

Helianthus tuberosus Zones 3–8.
Jerusalem artichoke tubers are a standby perennial crop for when the potatoes fail; they are sweet flavoured but not very popular with most people as they give you wind. But they make a quick screen and, being related to sunflowers, get on with sweet corn. The variety 'Fuseau' suppresses ground elder and equisetum. In the US, where they grow quite vigorously, they may themselves require suppressing or they could become a persistent weed.

Pastinaca sativa
Parsnips are slow to germinate; radishes are often sown with them to mark the spot and are removed before the parsnips need the space. Fresh seed must be used every year. They grow well with lettuce and peas if not shaded too much. The flowers attract hoverflies and predatory wasps and can be used as a sacrificial crop against carrot blossom moths.

Raphanus sativus
Radishes should not be grown only for their roots – the small seed pods are delicious. This crop needs to be grown

rapidly if it is to be edible. As radishes are distantly related to the brassicas they should usually be kept apart, though in seed-beds radishes attract pests such as flea beetles to themselves and may therefore be useful as a sacrificial crop. Radishes detest hyssop, but get on with most other plants except grapes and spinach. They benefit from the presence of nasturtium and mustard. Chervil, lettuce, peas and radishes all get on well together, though chervil is reputed to make radishes taste hot.

Scorzonera hispanica
Similar to salsify (see next entry) with long, thin, carrot-like roots, this may help repel carrot root fly; the flowers certainly benefit insects.

Tragopogon porrifolius
Salsify also has long, thin, carrot-like roots. It may grow well with watermelons and mustard, and discourage carrot root fly. The attractive flowers are beneficial to insects.

Carrot foliage protected by a wall of broad beans and leeks.

THE HERB GARDEN

Culinary herbs are more popular these days than they have ever been, though most people use only a few of the dozen or so commonly grown. Herbs are rich sources of vitamins and minerals and even if you don't want to eat them, you can absorb and enjoy them in the bath or dry them for potpourri. Their value for scenting the garden is dealt with on p. 105.

Parsley is so good for us that a garnish should go on every plate; grow and use chervil in combination with it for yet more goodness. Basil is so wonderful that once you have tried it fresh you will always grow it for use with almost every savoury dish! Rosemary, bay, sage, mint, chives and thyme are indispensable. Summer savory, dill and French tarragon have their uses. Whether you prefer dried oregano to fresh marjoram is up to you – either is delicious.

Few people use any other herbs more than very occasionally, but the following are all worth trying: angelica, bergamot, borage, chamomile, chervil, fennel, horseradish, hyssop, juniper berries, lemon balm, lovage, pot marigold, mugwort, rose geranium, salad burnet, winter savory, sorrel, sweet cicely, lemon verbena. The flowers of pot marigold, nasturtium, rose, rosemary, marrows and courgettes (zucchini) and day lily (*Hemerocallis*) can all brighten up salads.

Herbs for bathing

Much nicer than solvent-extracted bath oil is to run the bath water through a 'teabag' of fresh or dried herbs. An old pillowcase or even a stocking will stop you being bothered by leafy floaters. Try angelica, chamomile, chervil, elderflower, lemon balm, lemon verbena, lovage, mints, rosemary, sage and thyme.

Strewing herbs

These were popular before carpets and vacuum cleaners – they add scent, kill pests, are pleasant underfoot and let dirt through so that it falls beneath. Unfortunately they are a real fire risk. Pot-pourris of dried herbs can be stationed around the home and office to give pleasure without the risk. If you are a non-smoker, some places may be suitable for strewing – I have a lavender mulch on the floor of my car, and as I drive the scent helps me remain calm and tranquil. The more agitated the driving, the more my feet disturb the lavender, which then gives off more soothing scent. In the root cellar and on the floor of the potting shed the stems of mints and other herbs make a scented reminder of summer on a cold winter's day.

You can use any herbs you like for strewing or pot-pourri, but to repel fleas, mosquitos or other pests in the house you will have to use the less pleasing ones such as pennyroyal, rue, sage, santolina, southernwood, tansy or wormwood.

A glorious herb bed – chives, bergamot, sage,
French lavender and thyme.

Growing herbs

Herbs are often excellent companions and can therefore usefully be planted in many parts of the garden. The annual herbs are most conveniently grown with the vegetables, but the perennials have to be confined to the border. We have developed the habit of grouping the latter in a herb bed, conveniently situated near the kitchen, as they mostly prefer the same conditions of low fertility, free drainage, shelter and full sun. Wormwood, rue and possibly fennel are bad for each other and most other species, so should be omitted or confined with other irritant or poisonous plants like the euphorbias and castor oil plant. Finocchio fennel is an exception to this rule and can safely be grown in with other herbs, vegetables or saladings.

Irises are tough plants, not damaged by the secretions of wormwood (Artemisia absinthium) whose silver foliage has just crept in at the bottom of this picture.

Achillea millefolium Zones 3–9.
Yarrow has often been grown in herb borders as it helps oil production and vigour in other herbs and plants. It may be beneficial to animals and increases the overall fodder value of perennial ryegrass (*Lolium perenne*). It also accumulates phosphorus, calcium and silica. Yarrow is a very good and long-flowering host to hoverflies, ladybirds and predatory wasps.

Allium schoenoprasum Zones 3–9.
Chives are the most attractive of the alliums and are easy to divide and propagate. They are probably the best to grow to keep fungal diseases down. Use them against blackspot on roses and scab on apples, but be patient as it takes three years for them to have any real effect. They discourage aphids, particularly on chrysanthemums, sunflowers and tomatoes, and benefit carrots. Chive sprays have been used against downy and powdery mildew on cucumbers and gooseberries.

Anethum graveolens
Dill is an annual supposed to attract bees, though I find otherwise. It is said not to be liked by carrots, but there is conflicting opinion on this, too. It certainly aids cabbages, and may help lettuce, onions, sweet corn and cucumber. It repels aphids, slugs and spider mites, and attracts hoverflies.

Angelica archangelica or *A. officinalis*
Zones 4–8.
Angelica is no longer very popular for culinary use, but it is still grown commercially for flavouring. The oil content is improved if nettles are nearby.

Anthriscus cerefolium
Chervil is an annual that likes the shade, needs moisture and loathes being transplanted. It helps radishes (though they rarely need it in my experience!), but it is also reputed to make them hotter in flavour; it keeps ants and aphids off lettuces and is believed to repel slugs.

Armoracia rusticana Zones 4–8.
Horseradish may aid potatoes, but as it is almost impossible to get rid of it is best grown in large pots so that it can't escape. The pots can be half-buried in the potato bed. The perforated stainless steel drums that come out of washing machines make perfect confining tubs. According to Gerard horseradish is bad for grapes, but I suspect this is not the case. Horseradish accumulates calcium, potassium and sulphur. In the US it has been used against blister beetles and Colorado beetles. Planted under plum trees it helps protect them from curculios. The tea has been used against brown rot in apples. Mixed with garlic, chilli, mustard and cider vinegar it makes a warming sauce!

Artemisia spp.
This genus contains many plants with strong insecticidal properties and most have attractive filigree or silver foliage.

A. absinthium, wormwood, zones 3–9, is the strongest and most effective but also gives off exudations that inhibit other plants and can severely reduce yields. It is detested by many plants, especially the brassicas, and hinders caraway, fennel and sage. It does supply nectar for bees and hoverflies and discourages a variety of pests, including cats and dogs. The spray has been used against most pests. Do not put wormwood on the compost heap as it may slow it down.

A. abrotanum, southernwood, zones 5–8, is a delightful relative of wormwood that discourages moths and insects. It has a lovely scent of lemony pine. It is not as universally disliked as wormwood, so can be used in borders as a pest deterrent, particularly for brassicas and carrots. The US fruit tree moth can also be discouraged by southernwood.

A. dracunculus, tarragon, zones 5–9, is a culinary herb. Unfortunately the inferior Russian variety is propagated by seed and the better French, *A.d. Sativa*, only by root cuttings, so the former is more common and the herb is not appreciated as it deserves to be. Tarragon is delicious in all sorts of dishes and the leaves soaked in vinegar make a divine basis for salad dressing.

A. vulgaris, mugwort, is the wild form and supposed to benefit chickens.
   All the artemisias may be best confined to a corner away from other plants.

Borago officinalis
One of the best bee plants, borage is a good accumulator of minerals for compost and grows well with strawberries. It is an annual and can be used to reduce attacks of Japanese beetles and tomato hornworms.

Carum carvi
Caraway is deep rooted but difficult to establish. A biennial, hardy to zone 3, it has been suggested as a successor to peas in a crop rotation. If they are sown together, the caraway germinates once the peas are cleared and the ground harrowed. I suspect this only works with a long growing season – in the UK there would not be enough time for the two crops to mature one after the other. The flowers attract beneficial insects and the roots improve heavy soil.

Coriandrum sativum
An annual, coriander repels aphids and has been used as a spray against spider mites. It attracts bees but repels carrot root fly. It helps germinate anise but hinders seed setting in fennel, which itself hinders most plants – so coriander can be a good or a bad companion, depending how you feel about fennel. The seeds are the part most commonly used, added to bread or other baked dishes.

Foeniculum vulgare Zones 5–9.
Fennel has pretty, feathery leaves and is often grown as an annual, more for decoration than because it is useful. It has an inhibitory effect on beans, caraway, kohlrabi and tomatoes, and dislikes coriander and (like almost every other plant) wormwood. Fennel is a good host to hoverflies and predatory wasps and may deter aphids. The Italian variety finocchio has an edible swollen base and the stems are pleasant and refreshing to chew. Unlike many herbs, fennel needs rich, *moist* conditions.

Hyssopus officinalis Zones 3–9.
Hyssop is a perennial with little household use but it is a superb bee plant and makes lovely honey. It benefits grapevines and is helpful against the cabbage butterfly, but radishes do badly near it.

Lovage and red sage flank the view up the path to this magnificent bronze fennel at Lavenham Priory in Suffolk.

Laurus nobilis Zones 7–9.
Bay makes a small tree if not cut back by wind and frost. The leaves preserve grains and seeds from weevils. Burning leaves are poisonous to us and insects. Laurels have been said to be bad for grapes but precisely which species (or even genus) this applies to is not recorded.

Lavandula angustifolia Zones 5–9.
Lavender is a traditional way of keeping pests out of clothes but it also keeps them away from the garden. Try growing cotton lavender (*Santolina chamaecyparissus*, zones 6–8) and Russian lavender (*Perovskia*, zones 5–9) as well – they are unrelated but beneficial, especially to bees and other friends. *Lavandula stoechus* or French lavender is wonderfully aromatic but not very hardy (zones 8-9). All bring in bees and butterflies in late summer.

Levisticum officinale Zones 3–7.
Lovage adds flavour to vegetable stocks and is said to substitute for salt. A big plant, it likes moist soil and aids most other plants by its presence.

Marrubium vulgare Zones 3–8.
Horehound is a wild herb of chalky places and was once used medicinally. In the companion garden it stimulates and aids fruiting in tomatoes.

Matricaria recutita. Wild or German chamomile, also known as scented mayweed, is an annual. It is a good friend to wheat, but only when in small proportion. Cabbages and onions benefit from the

presence of a few chamomile plants nearby, improving both in yield and flavour. This chamomile accumulates potassium, calcium and sulphur and is host to hoverflies and wasps.

M. recutita has traditional medicinal as well as companion effects. It increases oil production from plants like peppermint and stimulates composting and yeasts. The extract increases the growth of yeasts even when diluted to one part in eight million.

Because of the long-standing confusion between this plant and the perennial *Chamaemelum nobile* or *Anthemis nobilis*, Roman or lawn chamomile, which is hardy to zone 4, it is possible that these remarks apply to both species.

Melissa officinalis Zones 4–8.
Lemon balm has an exquisite lemon scent. It benefits almost everything and should be in every part of every garden, particularly by gates and entrances where you can brush against it.

Mentha spp.
Mints love rich, moist soil, detest wood ash and are more than a little invasive. Plant them in pots buried in the soil to minimize their expansionist tendencies.

One of the few plants to grow under walnuts, mints also thrive near stinging nettles and help cabbage and tomatoes. The odour can be used to repel rodents, flies, clothes moths, fleas and flea beetles; spearmint also discourages aphids by discouraging their 'owners', the ants. Sprays of mint tea repel ants and Colorado beetle. Mints are wonderful autumn bee plants which also aid hoverflies and predatory wasps.

M. piperita Zone 3.
Peppermint oil is much used for its scent and flavour. Production is improved by the presence of stinging nettles; with chamomile it is reduced, but that of the chamomile is increased. Like most of this genus, it will help keep brassicas free of cabbage white butterfly caterpillars. It is loved by bees and other beneficial insects.

M. pulegium Zone 6.
Pennyroyal is beneficial to brassicas and has been used as a personal, household and garden insect repellent since time immemorial.

145

Monarda didyma Zones 4–9.
Bergamot is a pleasantly scented herb once drunk as Oswego tea and unrelated to the citrus bergamot used in Earl Grey tea. It will discourage flea beetles; strew bits amongst susceptible crops such as brassica seedlings.

Nepeta cataria not mussinnii Zones 3–8.
Catnip is extremely useful for driving away fleas and ants if you can stand the smell yourself. Most cats love it, so plant it where you want them to lurk. A patch near the strawberries can really keep down bird damage. If you are bothered by cats on your warm patio, put a bed of catnip in a hidden sunny spot and they will soon gravitate there. The scent helps repel aphids, flea beetles and in the US Colorado beetles, darkling beetles, Japanese beetles, squash bugs and weevils.

Ocimum basilicum
Basil is one of the tastiest herbs in the garden; it is just a shame that it needs so much warmth. It grows well and tastes delicious with tomatoes, and they are both happy with asparagus. It is thought to dislike rue. It can be used as a spray against asparagus beetle and as a trap plant for aphids. It also repels flies and mosquitos.

Origanum spp.
All the species of this genus are very beneficial and have strong aromatic oil that makes them favourites in the kitchen, either as marjoram or as oregano. The golden form of marjoram turns yellow when the sun is warm and bright enough and makes a cheerful and useful groundcover, heralding summer.

Petroselinum hortense Zone 3.
Parsley is the health-giving herb. A biennial, it loves rich, moist soil and is difficult to establish or move. Let it self-seed where it will. It aids most varieties of tomatoes and the two combine with asparagus to make a happy trio, but only if enough water is present. It has often been used to mask carrots and onions from their root flies, though it suffers from the carrot fly itself. It has been sprayed as a tea against asparagus beetles. Like dill, it is supposed to be loved by bees, but I find it attracts more hoverflies. Grown under roses it will repel their aphis.

Pimpinella anisum
Anise is a pungent annual, used in cooking and in ointments against insects, their bites and stings. Germination, seed formation and vigour improve when it is sown with coriander. A host plant to predatory wasps, it deters aphids and reduces cabbage worm attacks.

Rosmarinus officinalis Zones 7–9.
Rosemary is a not very hardy small shrub. It is valuable to us, bees and plants, but seeds will not germinate underneath it. Generally useful in the garden as its scent confuses many pests.

Ruta gravaeolens Zones 3–9.
Rue is a hardy perennial with attractive blue foliage which is very irritant in hot weather. It gets on badly with basil, but likes and is liked by figs. The smell will drive away fleas and Japanese beetles. A useful pest deterrent, rue is generally a good influence on other plants.

Salvia officinalis Zones 4–9.
Sage is a large shrub that aids and cooks well with the brassicas and carrots, protecting brassicas from many pests. It inhibits cucumbers, gets on well with rosemary and dislikes rue.

Santolina chamaecyparissus Zones 6–8.
Cotton lavender has been made into a spray against corn wireworms and southern rootworms. It makes a good edging for paths and the pervasive scent confuses pests.

Satureja montana Zones 4–9.
Winter savory is perennial, summer savory *S. hortensis* is an annual which grows and cooks well with broad beans and protects them from blackfly and beetles. It also gets on well with onions. Either summer or winter savory – it has not been established which – may be useful against Mexican bean beetles.

Symphytum officinale Zones 3–8.
Comfrey is used for poultices, ointments for skin conditions and internally against arthritis. It accumulates potassium, calcium and phosphorus, and has very high protein levels. Easy to grow in wet spots, it will extract nutrients from foul water. It will reduce scab on potatoes if handfuls of the wilted leaf are put in with the sets. Comfrey leaves rotted in a barrel make an excellent concentrated liquid feed, though it smells awful. Diluted down approximately twenty to one it is ideal for tomatoes and pot plants.

Purple sage backed by angelica and false valerian (Centranthus ruber).

Tanacetum vulgare Zone 3.
Tansy is a very strongly scented, yellow-headed herb traditionally used for ants – maybe it should be Antsy. The dried herb deters clothes moths and other household pests. Tansy accumulates potassium and is very beneficial in orchards. It gets on with most of the berries, roses and grapes, and is a host plant to ladybirds. The spray has been used against aphids, cabbage worms, squashbugs, Colorado beetles, Japanese beetles and striped cucumber beetles.

Thymus spp. Zones 3–9 depending on variety. Thymes are short lived and there are many rarely grown varieties such as the caraway-scented *T. herba barona* (zones 4–9) and the golden 'Anderson's gold'. Very good for us in the kitchen, it is also wonderful in the garden for bees! Thyme teas have been used to deter cabbage loopers, cabbage worms and whiteflies.

Tropaeolum majus
Nasturtiums are edible annuals, so can be used to enliven salads. They do best on poor soil. The strong smell drives woolly aphids off apple trees and keeps aphids and bugs away from broccoli and squash. Nasturtiums are themselves attacked by black aphids and cabbage caterpillars, so can be used as sacrificials, especially for tomatoes and beans. They keep whitefly out of greenhouses and off brassicas and are generally helpful to radishes, potatoes, brassicas and cucurbits.

Valeriana officinalis Zone 3.
Valerian is often confused with red valerian (*Centranthus ruber*, zones 5–8) and it can be difficult to tell which a book is referring to, so try both; *Centranthus ruber* is the easier to grow. One of the generally helpful and beneficial plants good for insect friends, cats and earthworms, valerian stimulates composting and accumulates phosphorus. Valerian tea used to be used to encourage flowering in fruit trees.

LIVESTOCK

Although breeding animals is usually considered only on smallholdings, anyone who would have a cat or dog can keep other creatures too. Most of them will be content to convert our surpluses and wastes into eggs, meat or entertainment, creating fertility all the while.

Chickens are good companions in the orchard, eating pests and spreading fertility. Very easy to look after, Bantam varieties give more beaks and eyes per pound of bird fed and are thus more efficient, but require better fencing. Their droppings are the best compost activator and more valuable to the gardener than their eggs. Chickens love the leaves of brassicas, and the leaves and seeds of beet and chard. They also supposedly like mugwort (the seed?) – it may help control their lice and worms.

Ducks are not as damaging in the garden as chickens and are far better for slug control. Muscovies are excellent for keeping with livestock as they control flies. Don't be put off by imagining that you have to have a lake – ducks do not need water to swim in, only to drink.

Geese are the best green lawnmowers, but they are noisy, eat the daffodils, strip the bark off young twigs, devour your carrot crop and steal all your windfall apples before you can get to them. They are very good at destroying buttercups and can be used to clear them from pasture, but encourage plantains which will need hand weeding.

Rabbits can easily be kept in hutches or mobile runs; they make good pets and efficient green lawnmowers. However, if they escape, they may do a lot of damage to almost any plant in the garden.

Horses, goats, sheep and cows produce lovely manures and are good green lawnmowers, though four-legged pets take much more investment and looking after than others. Animals will select the plants they need but can pick up bad food habits just like us. Clear their pasture of ragweed, bracken, larkspur and other poisonous weeds. Hedge garlic and similar strong-flavoured weeds will taint milk. Despite the fact that rue is poisonous, it used to be grown near stables to keep away flying pests, though it is unclear whether this means that horses are not susceptible to rue or that they were always kept under supervision when it was growing nearby.

Geese are truly green lawnmowers.

CHAPTER 7

BEING A GOOD COMPANION

As I have stressed throughout this book, companion planting is a weak effect easily outweighed by factors that have a more immediate impact. No amount of careful mixing or positioning is going to stop plants dying during a long drought, but the right companions will delay or lessen the damage. Companion planting is only one among many techniques of ensuring healthy plants: it cannot be taken in isolation. These other methods have to be mastered and understood so that they can work in unison with the companion effects, and the choice of the best method to employ changes as more emphasis is placed on companion planting.

Take weed control, for example: keeping the soil bare with hoeing and herbicides used to be considered good practice. From the contemporary, organic viewpoint this treatment is either harmful or at best far less helpful than covering the soil with a mulch. The benefits of mulching can be further augmented by block planting and intercropping with companion plants so that the leaves form a light-excluding canopy, thus starving out any weeds that manage to emerge from the mulch. These companion plants have to be chosen carefully so that they do not function as weeds competing with the crop; they should also provide for pollinators and predators.

All areas of gardening are modified when the companion approach is used, with broader mixtures of plants everywhere and many introduced specifically to attract wildlife. The main aim is to increase the overall level of life in the garden. This means having sacrificial and trap plants which will by definition sustain damage and may become unsightly. Careful planning will enable you to screen afflicted plants and prevent them being an eyesore.

But no amount of companion planting will compensate for plants badly grown, overcrowded or in the wrong position. First and foremost we have to learn to be good companions to our plants and to see to all their needs; only then can we reap the benefits of their interplay. Grow plants well using good techniques and they will respond with fruit and flowers.

This chapter concentrates on the primary importance of some basic gardening practices.

Creeping thyme can be used in place of weeding or mulching. Once established, thyme is one of the best choices for any companion planting design. It is low maintenance, suppresses weeds and gives the benefits of a mulch; it also feeds beneficial insects and provides shelter and cover for small predators. The striking variegated plant is a comfrey, Symphytum x uplandicum *'Variegatum'.*

Painting this wall white has lightened the garden and highlighted the lovely flowers of this 'Blue Azure' clematis.

AIR, LIGHT AND WATER

These are the three most important factors for plant growth – without them there is none. Some plants need more light than others, but this is only a matter of degree – in general the more light you can get into your garden, the better. In small gardens with high walls paint the surfaces white so that the light is reflected inside. Heavy shade from overhanging trees is compounded by their sucking away nutrients and moisture, so correct for this or growth will be severely limited.

Plants that prefer less direct sun or light shade are dealt with on p. 70. All vegetables do better in full sun providing there is sufficient moisture, though in drier conditions saladings may do better in the shade of taller crops. Combining plants of different heights succeeds in both the flower garden and the productive areas if care is taken not to let one choke the other at an early stage. Many companions of different heights can support each other in beds, sharing the light more or less equally while their root systems tap different levels of soil. A mono-crop will present a smaller, flatter surface to the sun and all the roots will be at the same level.

If sufficient light can reach most leaves of a plant, air can probably circulate freely. This is far more important than many of us realize. If new air cannot reach the leaves they cannot absorb carbon dioxide and no photosynthesis or growth will occur. The availability of carbon dioxide can be increased by having more animal life, large or small; under cover, try fermenting wine or beer in bottles amongst the plants to enrich the air when growth is strong and ventilation limited early in the year.

Poor air circulation will make many plants much more prone to mildews and other fungus problems, aggravated if there is a shortage of moisture at the roots. Gales, draughts and strong winds are also undesirable and the balance between sufficient shelter against these and enough openness to allow air to move freely is dependent on planning and discreet pruning.

Water is usually the easiest of the three basic needs to supply. It is difficult to control the others, but water comes out of a hose in almost unlimited quantities. Except, of course, when we need it most – in a drought. It is then that the efforts of the good gardener reap their rewards.

The higher humus content in organically well-tended soils retains more moisture from the rainy periods than chemically fertilized soils which have burned off their organic matter. Mulches further increase the water holding by stopping it evaporating and layers of plants with different levels of leaves trap moisture as it tries to escape or replace it as dew.

When watering, apply the same philosophy as with fertility. We feed the soil, not the plants and we should water the soil, not the plants. Wet leaves are rarely beneficial – high humidity may be good for some plants such as melons, but water on leaves frequently just causes more risks of damage and infection.

Very cold water may harm tiny tender seedlings in a propagator, but otherwise there is no advantage to be had from warm water. Stagnant water from a dirty, ill-sited butt may harbour pests and disease and should not be used on young seedlings; on the other hand, tap water may contain too many chemicals for them. Fresh, clean rainwater is therefore the best and every effort should be made to catch and store each drop.

It is best to water plants under cover in the morning so that they have plenty to draw on during the heat of the day; in the hottest weather, watering several times a day may be necessary. Do not worry about burning the leaves with drops of water in the midday sun, as this rarely happens. Conversely, it is not a good idea to make them cold and damp by watering last thing at night, but this is better than leaving them to wilt.

In open ground it is important to water thoroughly some time before sowing or planting so that the excess water has a chance to drain away. Waterlogging is bad for seeds and roots: it kills from lack of air and there is almost nothing worse than a thick, heavy mud congealing all around them. When rain is short, an occasional heavy watering is far better than watering little and often. The latter makes roots come to the surface where they form an ineffective mat. Infrequent but thorough waterings soak the lower layers of soil and the plants follow, rooting down and chasing after the water. Sprinklers are more wasteful than trenches or trickle hoses, which deliver water under the plants without spraying it everywhere merely to evaporate.

The shade and drought under large trees is a serious handicap to those vegetables trying to grow there.

If a particular spot needs regular watering, this is going to be done far more often if you make the task less arduous. It is easy and not very expensive to run permanent hosepipes to the greenhouse and every part of the garden. Quick connectors allow a short delivery hose to be joined in where needed. The time saved in not hauling about cans or long lengths of hose is increased by reduction in damage done by the hose decapitating seedlings, flowers etc.

A riot of colour. The open effect indicates good air circulation and thus less risk of mildews and moulds.

BREAKING NEW GROUND

Once you have planned your garden, you may need to make beds out of 'virgin' soil. Turning weedy ground into clean soil is one of the most important jobs in gardening; it is also one of the hardest, but it can be made easier. After a couple of years laid down as close-cut grass, the top layer of turf can be stripped off or dug in and will leave very clean soil with few weeds to be eradicated. If the sward is very rough with many deep-rooted weeds, this method becomes harder work as they keep recurring and need frequent hoeing. Spreading weeds that reroot in each piece of turf are even more of a problem and worst where rotivators are used. These chop weeds into many more little bits while sadly doing the same to much of the soil life. Bringing these weeds under control before sowing or planting is essential, as they will take much more time and labour to eradicate once the bed has been planted up.

The traditional method of digging out roots and hoeing regularly will work well if you are prepared to put in plenty of time and effort, but is best on small areas only. On a larger scale it becomes impractical. Herbicides will kill most weeds quickly, making your task easier, but you will probably prefer to avoid these, especially on land that is to be used for crops. Herbicides pollute the soil, kill invisible plant life and damage many other forms of microlife. Organic standards for commercial growers forbid their use, and we should all follow these guidelines. Using a flame gun to get rid of established weeds is also ecologically undesirable, as burning off the top growth wastes useful material and leaves only the ash. It is, however, an efficient way of eliminating swathes of little seedlings in wet springs and of keeping paths and drives clean.

The easiest method of breaking ground is to use a light-excluding, heavy mulch to choke out the weeds. Mark out the proposed bed and dig a slit trench 30 cm (1 ft) or less deep and wide all round the inside of this edge. Spread the soil into any low spots and raze bumps to make it all level. Cover the whole bed during March or April with old carpet, wet newspapers, cardboard or underfelt. Plastic sheeting is less good for several reasons; it can be used as a last resort but must be absolutely light-proof. The cover can be made neat and tidy with a sprinkling of shredded bark, leaf mould, peat or grass clippings. The weeds die from lack of light and the warm, moist conditions rot down their remains into fertility. Clear the cover away in the autumn and the area can be forked over and prepared for planting. All the weeds will have gone and the soil will be in a much better, more friable condition.

If any weeds make it through the mulch, they must be pulled out, but they rarely do. What is more, if the mulch goes on in March, the weeds should be sufficiently under control to allow plants like tomatoes, courgettes (zucchini) and brassicas to be carefully planted through holes in the mulch in May.

To dig or not to dig

This is a perpetual argument among gardeners. On the whole the best plan is to dig over the ground initially and perhaps once a decade thereafter. The benefits of annual digging are too small to make such a chore worthwhile; the same effort can be put to better use for turning the compost. Obviously some crops such as potatoes need digging out, and planting holes have to be dug for trees. 'No-diggers' merely avoid the regular autumnal dig, claiming that it destroys the natural strata of the soil and chops up many friends like worms, and that the disturbance tends to unearth more weed seeds. Digging is only essential if the soil gets badly packed down, but this can be avoided by not walking on the soil when it is wet and using fixed or raised beds with permanent pathways (see p. 129).

Fertilizers

As explained earlier (see p. 38), soluble chemical fertilizers should be avoided and efforts made to boost the soil life instead. All soils will benefit from a monthly handful of fresh grass clippings scattered over each square metre (square yard) or so to feed and encourage the worms. Well-rotted manures and garden compost are too valuable and in too short supply for most of us to dig them in or spread them widely, but they should be well mixed in with the soil whenever anything is being planted.

The best manures are working horse, pet horse and milking cow. Fattening bullock manure and pig slurries have less value and contain many more pollutants. Donkeys, goats and sheep produce poorer quality dung but it is still a useful resource and should be mixed into compost heaps. For reasons of hygiene, cat, dog and human droppings are best disposed of or deep-pit composted for a three-year period before incorporating them in the soil. Urine is relatively safe, but must be diluted by between ten and twenty to one before you put it on the soil or use it as a compost activator. Ideally, local laws permitting, use it on grassed areas to encourage the sward – the extra clippings then make more mulching material for elsewhere.

Bird droppings are one of the richest of all manures, but can burn plant leaves and roots, so they should never be used fresh. Mixed into compost heaps they will really help them heat up – they are more effective at this than almost any other stimulant. Feathers are also quickly converted and are another rich source of fertility.

Ground rock dusts are slow at releasing nutrients and take several years to show full benefits, though they are slightly quicker in organically rich soils. They are relatively sustainable and are frequently an otherwise wasted byproduct of mining. Ground lime for calcium has been used for centuries; Dolomitic lime contains more magnesium, so is preferred by most gardeners if they can get it. Calcified seaweed is a lime made from seaweed deposits and is the best, as it contains a wider range of trace elements. Ground rock potash and phosphate are useful, especially if a veganic approach requires all animal sources of the latter to be dropped. Rock potash is needed more on light than on heavy soils and as it is so inexpensive it should be used extravagantly. Potash is soon lost from light soils and any shortage will badly affect the health and cropping of many plants. Wood ashes are another source of potash, but are usually scarce and therefore best reserved for the potassium-hungry gooseberries and cooking apples.

As well as major nutrients, seaweed products, dried and calcified seaweed all contain trace elements in a natural, slow-release form and are a sustainable resource. They have a gentle action and are widely preferred as the best source of imported fertility. The regular use of seaweed extract makes plants more resistant to pests and diseases and stimulates the life in the soil.

A liquid feed for plants in pots and for encouraging transplants was traditionally made by hanging a sack of manure in a butt of water. This is best replaced by comfrey solution. Comfrey leaves are gathered and mixed with nettles and herbs, packed down into a container and just covered with water and urine. After a few weeks, a vile, smelly black liquid can be poured off. Diluted down it is similar to commercial tomato feed and can be used in the same way.

Green manuring

Rotation and green manures are better ways of improving the soil than importing fertility. Green manures require an initial input of seeds but afterwards can mostly be raised from self-saved seed, making the garden almost self-sufficient in fertility. Most green manures are expressly grown for material to augment fertility, though like any groundcover crops they reduce leaching and soil erosion, aid microlife and convert sunlight to plant material. Like crops used in rotation they act as companion plants over time, aiding plants that come after them. Whenever a plant is removed, most of its roots and root hairs are left to break down in the soil. Some, such as the legumes, also leave their rhizomatic partners behind – these are then a very rich source of nutrients to following plants. All plants continually produce leaf litter and most accumulate more dust, debris and insect remains than bare soil.

Green manures are chosen for their reliable production of materials and for the ease with which they are afterwards incorporated into the soil. As most green manures are quick to establish and strongly competitive they are not grown with crops; instead they are usually sown after the crops have been harvested and left to grow through the winter months when the ground would otherwise be vacant. Many weeds would similarly grow through the winter and accumulate more valuable materials than most green manures, but they would also be much more difficult to eradicate when the time came. Green manures may be dug in before the next crop is planted, pulled or hoed off and composted, grazed by the livestock or lawnmower or covered in a sheet mulch as suggested under *Breaking new ground* (see p. 152).

Whichever method of incorporation you choose, allow time for the decomposition to proceed and any regrowth of the green manure to be destroyed before planting out the crop: a poor result may follow if this precaution is not taken. The period for initial decomposition depends on season, soil, plant and method, but at least a week or two will be needed.

The choice of green manure depends on many factors which limit the practical range of plants that can be used. Companion effects are important and a sowing of several green manures will give better results than a single one. Crop and related plants are not often used as it is then difficult to fit them into a rotation; otherwise, most plants can be grown simply to compost and return to the soil as extra fertility. Weeds are a free source and often accumulate minerals less available to crop plants. The plants are most valuable before the flowers have set seed and/or the stems and leaves have dried and hardened. Any invasive plants such as couch grass can be withered in the sun for a few days before composting.

PLANTS GROWN MAINLY FOR BULK OR COMPOST

These plants are valuable on their own but do even better grown in mixtures containing legumes. Many may also be grown as intercrops (see p. 30).

Brassica napus
Oil seed rape. Height 1.2–1.5 m (4–5 ft). A brassica, and probably the best for bulk. It is loved by bees and can be sown in midsummer if there is enough moisture for it to germinate. It will also stand the winter. It is, of course, related to the brassicas grown as vegetables, and therefore not suited to crop rotations involving them.

Fagopyrum esculentum
Buckwheat. Height 60 cm (2 ft). Pink flowers beloved by hoverflies make this a must for companion planting, but buckwheat also makes a good green manure even in poor soils. Unfortunately it is not winter hardy. Sow April to August.

Helianthus annuus
Sunflower. Height 30 cm (1 ft) or more. Easy to grow but must not be allowed to form heads. It will produce a lot of bulk from a late spring start and can follow winter brassicas or leeks. Cucurbits or sweet corn can be interplanted and cropped while the sunflowers are cut for compost. Unrelated to any of the commonly rotated plants, sunflowers are especially useful as grow-your-own stakes. Sow April to August.

Impatiens glandulifera
Himalayan balsam. Height 90 cm–1.2 m (3–4 ft). This has become a weed of wet places and self-seeds about the garden, but I find it a useful quick crop to grow from early spring. It is easy to pull and produces great bulk of very easily compostable stems like those of busy lizzie (*Impatiens*). It is killed by cold weather, so sow April to August if moist.

Limnanthes douglasii
Poached egg plant. Height 45 cm (18 in). This does not give much bulk on the surface, though it has extensive root growth. However it is a superb bee and hoverfly attractant, will grow through most winters and is easy to incorporate after flowering. Not related to rotated plants, it is especially useful under soft fruit and shrubs. Sow April to September.

Phacelia tanacetifolia
Height 90 cm (3 ft). Grown in the ornamental garden for its pretty blue flowers, this feathery plant produces a good tilth with masses of fine roots. It is shallow rooted but easy to grow and incorporate; it also attracts dew, is beneficial while growing as an insect attractant and loved by bees. Sow April to August; it may overwinter and provide even earlier flowers for insects.

Secale cereale
Grazing (Hungarian) rye. Height 60 cm (2 ft). This is the best rye for the garden, though there are, of course, many varieties for use in the fields, where they are usually sown with legumes. Sow *S. cereale* from August to November for winter soil cover.

Sinapsis alba
Mustard. Height 60 cm (2 ft). Not a brassica as such but a member of the crucifer family (like the brassicas) and closely related to them. Gertrud Franck maintains that mustard's effects are wholly beneficial, that using it does not cause more clubroot (to which the brassicas are prone) and therefore it can be used without much regard to rotation effects. Much grown for green manure, it is shallow rooting but can still produce tremendous bulk from a midsummer sowing. It is loved by bees and other insects. Sow from March to September, as it is killed by hard frosts.

Spinacea oleracea
Spinach. Height 30 cm (1 ft). Very quick growing in moist soil, it is ideal for sheet composting, rotting down rapidly. Not related to most rotated crops, it can be interplanted and incorporated fairly continuously through the growing season. Sow March to September, avoiding midsummer in hot climates.

LEGUMES

The chief benefit of legumes is that they add nitrogen to the soil, as their roots harbour mycorrhizal bacteria and fungi which fix it from the air. They may be grown on their own or mixed with other legumes and non-legumes; this last method produces more bulk but less immediate nitrogen as the action of the legume is suppressed by the other plant. Once all the material has been broken down, more fertility is available from the combination. Clovers are the best nitrogen fixers, and it is better to sow a mixture rather than a single variety.

Lupinus angustifolius
Bitter blue lupin. Height 60 cm (2 ft). The best conditioner for thin acid soils. An annual with deep roots, it deserves to be grown more often than it is. Sow March to June.

Medicago lupulina
Trefoil. Height 60 cm (2 ft). This is a good annual for light soils and is shade tolerant, so it makes a good undercrop, especially for sweet corn. It is short lived but hardy. Sow March to August.

Medicago sativa
Alfalfa or lucerne. Zone 5. Height 1.2 m (4 ft). A hardy perennial often included in mixtures for orchards or meadows, it can be grown as a short-term crop. It is deep rooted and drought resistant once established. It needs rhizobium companion bacteria when first grown, and liming is essential if the soil is acid. Sow April to July.

Melilotus alba
White sweet clover, yellow blossom or American sweet clover. Zone 3. Height 1.2–1.5 m (4–5 ft). Do not confuse this with *Trifolium repens*, below. Not a true clover, *M. alba* has the same benefits. It produces the most bulk of all and is winter hardy. It is very quick growing and thus competes too well when grown in most mixtures, though it is often included with kale and sunflowers to make a game-fowl-encouraging crop. Sow April to September.

Pisum sativum arvense
Field peas. Height 90 cm (3 ft). Any pea can be used to add fertility, but some have been bred for the purpose. One example is 'Marathon', a type of maple pea. Not winter hardy, it can produce a great bulk from a spring sowing, but in the garden it might be better to use and eat an edible variety or a vetch.

Trifolium hybridum
Alsike clover. Zone 3. Height 30 cm (1 ft). The clover to grow on wet acid soils, but lime these to make them sweet first. A hardy perennial, but, like most clovers, best grown for short periods. Sow April to August.

Trifolium incarnatum
Crimson clover. Height 60 cm (2 ft). Good for light soils, this is an annual clover loved by bees for its crimson flowers. Sow March to August.

Trifolium pratense
Altaswede. Zone 3. Height 45 cm (18 in). Not a swede but a red clover variety, longer lived and less prone to clover rot. It is slow to bulk, so more useful for grazing leys than for short-term green manure. The similar Essex red clover is commoner, a hardy perennial which loves rich, loamy soil; valuable to almost all beneficial insects, it deserves to be grown more widely. Sow March to August.

Trifolium repens
White clover. Zone 3. Height 30 cm (1 ft). Do not confuse this true clover sometimes known as sweet white with white sweet or American sweet clover which is *Melilotus alba* (see above). *T. repens* needs a firm seed-bed. As it is low growing and forms a good weed-suppressing cover, it is useful under fruit and shrubs. Produces less bulk than red clover, but better cover. Sow April to October.

Trigonella foenum-graecum
Fenugreek. Height 60 cm (2 ft). Not practical as a seed crop in the UK because of the long season it needs to mature, this annual makes a good green manure with rapid growth and should not be undersown in slower cropping mixtures. Produces tremendous bulk and is unrelated to most crops, so can be used in the vegetable garden without complications. Sow April to August, as it is killed by cold weather.

Vicia faba
Field bean. Height 60 cm–1.2 m (2–4 ft). Related to the broad bean, this is sweet smelling and good for honey as well as being very hardy (to zone 7 or 8). The haulm is excellent for bulking compost heaps. Sow September to November.

Vicia sativa
Winter tare or spring vetch. Height 75 cm (2 ft 6 in). This hardy annual or biennial (zone 5) makes good winter cover, best suited to heavy soil. Very vigorous and produces great bulk, but is usually sown with a cereal crop. *V. villosa*, hairy vetch, is similar but less dominating. Sow March to September.

MINERAL-ACCUMULATING PLANTS

As we have seen, weeds are often the best at this and thrive on soils short in those very elements. They can be made into teas, liquid feeds or sprays, but their best use is for composting. Pernicious weeds like couch grass can be withered before incorporation; seeding weeds should only be put in the middle of a heap expected to get hot.

The following minerals are essential to the health of many plants – and people – although some may be needed in only minute quantities (in which case they are known as trace elements).

Boron
Particularly needed in minute amounts by brassicas and apples, this is accumulated by the euphorbias or spurges.

Calcium
Lime. Earthworms make this available, so feed them with seaweed and grass clippings. Many plants, especially rhubarb, accumulate calcium as crystals of oxalate – these are poisonous and bitter, so they protect the plant from grazing animals.

Good accumulators of lime include: beech, brassicas, broom, buckwheat, cacti, coltsfoot, comfrey, corn chamomile, corn marigold, creeping thistle, daisies, dandelions, equisetum, fat hen, goose grass, melons, oak leaves and bark, okra, purslane, scarlet pimpernel, shepherd's purse, silverweed, stinging nettles.

Cobalt
One of the rarest elements, this is essential to animals but not to most plants. Fortunately it is concentrated for us by buttercups, comfrey, equisetum, ribbed plantain, rosebay willow herb, vetch.

Copper
Rather too readily supplied in pig muck, as it is added to their food. Plants growing on this may be poisoned. Otherwise, copper is generally in short supply, so welcome from buttercups, chickweed, coltsfoot, creeping thistle, dandelions, plantains, stinging nettles, thistles, vetch, yarrow.

Iron
Shortage of iron, or too much lime locking it up, causes chlorosis, the plant equivalent of anaemia. Iron is available from beans, buttercups, chickweed, chicory, coltsfoot, comfrey, creeping thistle, dandelions, equisetum, fat hen, foxgloves, ground ivy, groundsel, silverweed, stinging nettles.

Magnesium
Another element that may be locked up by lime, causing chlorosis. It is available from: beech, beet, chicory, coltsfoot, daisies, equisetum, larches, oaks, plantains, potatoes, salad burnet, silverweed, yarrow.

Manganese
May also be locked up by lime. Needed by the beets more than by other crops, this is found in buttercups, chickweed, comfrey.

Nitrogen
All of the following accumulate this, but only while young and succulent: beans, bindweed, black nightshade, broad-leaved dock, chickweed, clovers, comfrey, creeping thistle, dandelions, fat hen, grass clippings, groundsel, knotgrass, peas, purslane, sow thistle, stinging nettles, vetches, white campion, yarrow.

Any legume accumulates nitrogen, but with them it is mostly in the root system.

Phosphorus
Needed for good roots, this is an important ingredient in bonemeal, but the organic approach prefers to provide it naturally. Plants accumulating it are broad-leaved dock, buttercups, comfrey, corn marigold, fat hen, henbane, oak leaves, purslane, sheep sorrel, thornapple, vetch, yarrow.

Potassium
Needed for fruiting and disease resistance, especially by gooseberries and cooking apples. It is found in apple leaves, beech leaves, broad-leaved dock, buttercups, chickweed, chicory, coltsfoot, comfrey, corn chamomile, couch grass, fat hen, goose grass, maple leaves, plantains, purslane, stinging nettles, sunflowers, tansy, thistles, thornapples, tobacco, vetch, yarrow.

Silica
Makes plants tougher and more disease resistant. Best found in equisetum, but also in couch or knotgrass, onions, plantains, stinging nettles.

Sulphur
Important for disease resistance and found in the alliums and brassicas, coltsfoot, fat hen, horseradish, purslane.

Foxgloves accumulate iron and compost the flower stems and leaves before they set seed.

Weed Control

As explained earlier, weeds are the plants most suited to the conditions in a particular place, and they flourish at the expense of others. They may have their uses as soil enrichers and stabilizers, but most of the time we are rightly more concerned about their bad companion effects than about any benefits they may bring.

Weed control is like pest control – we need precise control, not total eradication. Perennial and established weeds in beds and borders need to be destroyed, as explained under *Breaking new ground*, p. 152, but in other places are useful groundcover and preferable to bare soil. Natural weeds like the willow herbs can be attractive and will look after themselves, requiring no time or attention. Nettle patches are a useful fertility and wildlife resource, while docks and thistles in pasture are deep-rooting pioneers, pulling up nutrients and making them available to shallower-rooting plants. The eradication of established perennial weeds leaves bare soil that needs more repetitive maintenance to prevent pernicious, self-seeding, annual weeds multiplying and spreading.

Bare soil is always best covered in thick mulches and then planted up with choice plants. Ground that is growing nothing is a wasted resource and just tempting weeds to return. Groundcover of sacrificial fruit or plants for beneficial insects is more useful to the rest of the garden than bare soil or some drab evergreen.

In the vegetable beds it is often difficult to keep the soil covered at all times and mulches may not be as practical for some crops as they are in other parts of the garden. Regular hoeing at fortnightly intervals will prevent any weeds becoming established and the small weedlings can be left to wither. Leaving a longer gap between hoeings gives the weeds time to grow bigger and more inclined to reroot, so they need to be collected. If a weed becomes established then fortnightly hoeings will not kill it – you will need to hoe once a week until it expires. The critical thing is not to let new leaves unfurl and replenish the root systems, but to weaken the plants continually by removing them as fast as they are produced.

On paths and patios, using a sharp knife is easier than pulling by hand, but for most situations a knife on the end of a stick – a hoe – is best. A very sharp hoe is an easy tool to use and a blunt one makes the job slow and unpleasant. Have a hoe with a thin, hard blade, sharpen it with a stone every twenty minutes or so and hoeing becomes pleasant work. Avoid stainless steel and cheap 'tin' hoes as they will not keep an edge – the best blades are made from a piece of old scythe.

Sowing

This is one of the most important techniques of all – get it wrong and the plants never appear. The single commonest problem is sowing too deep, so as a general rule sow less deeply, especially for the smallest seeds. Very few seeds germinate if covered with more than 2.5 cm (1 in) of soil. Large seeds have more food reserves and can emerge from greater depths (but are more likely to be eaten by animals and birds). Old seed may still be viable after many years: the larger seeds last better than the smaller, and parsley and

Wild, alpine and garden strawberries all make wonderful groundcover, benefiting insects with their flowers and shelter, and the birds and us with fruit.

parsnips keep for the shortest time. Try suspect seed indoors in a pot a few weeks early to see if it comes up before risking the entire effort. It is easy to save the seed of most plants yourself.

Different plants are sown in different ways for convenience and necessity. Tender plants are started off in a propagator, singly or multi-sown and pricked out, potted on, hardened off and planted out, while root vegetables are sown direct where they are to stand. However, those that are sown *in situ* make the best plants. Growing from the start in the soil, they are invariably stronger than plants grown by any other method – *if* they are not frosted, eaten or accidentally hoed while small. But because of these risks, it is much more reliable to sow in pots or a seed-bed and transplant later. This leaves the main beds clear for weeding and allows for inter- and catch cropping. The multi-celled plastic modules are excellent for this and using them makes for more accurate sowing and better protection of the seedlings.

Some plants need individual pots of a larger capacity and if space is available they benefit most. Brassicas and leeks always do well if started in a seed-bed and moved once *before* transplanting to their final position. The extra move at an early stage helps them make a more fibrous rootball.

When sowing directly in the ground, water the hole or drill and let the water drain away before placing the seed. This ensures adequate moisture underneath the seed without forming a crust above. Use a mixture of peat and sand or similar sterile material to cover small seeds. There will then be minimal competition right next to the tiny seedling at the most critical time of its life. A dark mixture also marks the positions and warms the soil and seed.

If you are sowing indoors, be careful not to waterlog the compost or the seed will drown. Water from underneath by filling a tray and *drain it off* afterwards. Use only fresh water on seeds and seedlings as stagnant water butts harbour damping-off and wilt diseases.

HARDENING OFF

Hardening off is critical for plants leaving a protected environment and going out into the open garden. Any check to growth is bad for plants and will always reduce the final result, though the damage may not be obvious at the time. The chilling plants can receive if not hardened off may prevent them growing again for many weeks, if at all.

Hardy plants grown under cover need hardening off for three or four days: stand them outside during the day and return them under cover each night. They adapt bit by bit to the harsher conditions – not just the cold but the winds – and only then can they grow successfully when planted out. Some protection for a longer period after hardening off can only be of benefit and the more gradually any stages are employed the better.

The less hardy the plant, the longer the period of hardening off it will need and the more protection will help. Never put out any tender plants until you are sure the last frost has passed, harden them off for at least a week and continue to give them some protection until the nights are reliably warm.

For several years now lobelias have self-sown in this ornamental font – but they never make as good a display as if they are started off under cover in the warm and planted out.

Very much the same applies in reverse when plants are brought indoors for the winter. Do not bring them from the cool, moist garden to a hot, dry living room in one movement, but allow them to adapt gradually over a few days.

TRANSPLANTING

When transplanting always dig a hole twice as big as you think necessary, water the hole far more than you think necessary and firm the roots a bit more than you think necessary. If the plant is coming from indoors you should also harden it off for far longer than you think necessary.

Water the plant well the day before the operation and again immediately before. Water the hole copiously and let the water drain out of the hole before planting, as mud does not pack around roots properly. Mix compost with the soil before packing it around the roots and make sure they are spread out and not crowding each other. Firm it all in well (with small plants extremely well), then hold a leaf between finger and thumb and pull. If it tears, well and good, if it pulls the plant out it was not in firmly enough! Continue to water the new transplant religiously until new growth is visible.

MULCHING

Mulching is one of the best things you can do for most plants in the garden. Mulches keep moisture in the soil, aiding the microlife as well as the plants. This is augmented by a warming of the soil over the whole season. Although mulches initially keep the ground cooler, from late spring they are keeping the soil warmer by preventing nightly heat loss. Mulches of organic materials break down and require replenishment, but add much to the fertility in the process. The humus, gums and colloids formed improve the moisture-holding capacity and the texture of the soil.

Any mulch should only be put down on wet soil or following heavy rainfall, as it may prevent any further rain reaching the soil afterwards. A mulch can absorb its own depth of rain, in droughts interspersed with brief showers be careful to drag it aside before the rain starts and replace it afterwards.

Weed seeds will be prevented from germinating if they are buried under about 5 cm (2 in) of mulch. Because of the loose texture of the mulch, any weeds germinating within it will be easy to hoe or pull, but if they are allowed to establish they will be very tiresome. Existing weeds will benefit from mulches by as much or more than the crop plants, so be sure to eliminate them first. The only exception is where a heavy impenetrable sheet is used as the mulch.

A drawback of mulching is that no new material is created from the sunlight falling on ground that is covered. Large areas are better mulched and then filled with companion plants that do not compete with the main planting, but aid it and utilize its surplus light.

The best and most attractive mulches are the organic ones such as peat, leaf mould and shredded composted bark. These can be expensive or ecologically costly and are best saved for the more visible ornamental beds. Spent mushroom compost is not unattractive and rarely harbours many weed seeds. Straw, grass clippings, sawdust and newspaper are cheap and practical for fruit and vegetables and arranged with care need not be too unsightly. Even well-made garden compost is usually too full of weed seeds to use as a mulch and it is too valuable anyway. Well-rotted farmyard manure is more easily obtained in sufficient quantities to use as a mulch and is also the richest in fertilizer value: it is probably the best of all to use.

Inorganic materials like sand, gravel or pebbles are excellent for suppressing weeds and retaining moisture and should be more widely used. They are relatively cheap and last well; they are also attractive enough for ornamental beds, where their only drawback is that they make it more difficult to plant and fertilize. Sharp sand is most useful 2.5-5 cm (1-2 in) deep on top of heavy clay, where it is the easiest material to sow or plant through and makes hoeing a joy; when it gets dirty it can be dug in. Carpets, synthetic fabrics and plastic sheets are good for breaking new ground (see p. 152); once the garden is established they can be used in strips for pathways amongst soft fruit and vegetables.

Pine needles have a specific use in strawberry beds, where they discourage slugs and improve the flavour of the fruit while inhibiting weeds. They are of little help to other plants, though – coniferous material slows decomposition, inhibits germination and is best for paths or underneath the trees producing it.

Pest Control

Using companion planting will give good pest control by building up the natural predators and making healthier plants, but this takes time and it is always best to use a belt-and-braces approach at first if there are any severe problems. Although there are many safe and effective organic methods of direct action available, these are rarely required once the garden is well established.

Do not panic if a few pests or diseases appear – they are necessary to feed up the predators. Look to the general health of your plants first, not to individual attacks. If they appear to be doing well otherwise, you can either merely observe the course of the attack or take some relatively benign action. Try washing off pests with jets of water or boosting the plants with sprays of seaweed solution. Only use any pesticide sprays as a last resort.

Most plants can sustain a lot of apparent damage without it affecting the final yield. Loss of leaf area is a minor problem as lower leaves will then receive proportionately more light and the total amount will not vary much. Attacks by pests that remove under a quarter of an established plant's leaves can therefore be regarded as a minor problem needing action only to prevent it becoming worse. Many fruits are summer pruned, especially if they are trained as cordons, fans or espaliers. Over half the current year's growth is removed, making more fruit buds for the following year. The same function is performed by aphids, which

invariably attack soft young growth and wither the tips: this redirects the growth to forming fruit buds, thus saving the gardener work!

A spurious bit of reasoning concerns the spread of virus disease by aphids. It is true that the virus disease is spread by aphids, *but* in the same way that the rabies virus is spread by dogs – if a rabid dog bites you, putting it to death will not prevent you getting rabies! If aphids are

Chervil, dill and onions left to flower with a few self-sown poppies not weeded out and borage in the background. All these are excellent for bringing beneficial insects into the area, and these (or their offspring) then control pests.

already attacking your plants the damage is done, it is too late for spraying. Spraying under these circumstances may prevent the aphids increasing in number, but can hardly prevent infection. Only isolation in a fine net will give complete protection. Far better to encourage the natural predators to keep the numbers down by filling the garden with their companion plants.

Many pests and few friends travel up the trunks of trees and a sticky band of grease stops them. This can be made more effective if a trap is set below, by winding a strip of sacking round the trunk. Pests take it for bark and hide there, to be found and destroyed at our leisure. Mechanical barriers work exceedingly well. Net curtain will stop carrot fly laying its eggs on the crop, felt squares around young brassicas stop the cabbage root fly doing the same, net or stocking bags keep pests off fruit.

As mentioned above, jets of water can clear many pest problems. Tougher pests usually succumb to a spray of soft soap solution and for the really hard cases derris and pyrethrum may be needed. These are plant extracts believed harmless to mammals while killing insects, including bees! If needed, derris or pyrethrum should be used late at night so that they miss the bees and have time to be naturally deactivated by morning.

They also kill caterpillars so can be used against the troublesome gooseberry sawfly, though there are better sprays for cabbage caterpillars. *Bacillus thuriengiensis* is a naturally occurring disease of caterpillars and is harmless to most other forms of life. It can be sprayed on to cabbages and other brassicas to protect them from the white butterfly caterpillar with no danger to us or to the environment.

Read the instructions fully and take every precaution, as even gentle sprays may have some side effects. It is now a criminal offence in the UK to make, use or store a home-made pesticide – even the traditional boiled rhubarb leaves and soft soap is illegal.

Under cover, natural pest control is more difficult: it is very difficult to create enough life systems in a greenhouse or polytunnel to control pests. Toads and frogs and other friends can be given shelters under pots in damp corners. Ladybirds and other beneficial insects can be brought in, but without the diversity of plant life will not establish themselves. Companion plants such as marigolds will stop many pests coming under cover, but will not dislodge them once in. The use of soft soap and permitted sprays may be resorted to more frequently than outside, but over the last few years more natural predators have become available to amateurs. Red spider mite, whitefly, aphids, mealy bugs, scale insects, vine weevils and leaf miners can all be controlled by introducing large numbers of their predators. The packs of predators available commercially cost rather too much for a small private greenhouse, but shared among three they work out at less than the cost of a single spraying.

Before introducing predators (or spraying), try reducing levels of infestation with sacrificial plants. Red spider mites love broad beans more than most other plants and can be lured on to them if they are mixed in with the crops. Whiteflies are attracted to sweet tobacco and aphids to basil. Once the pests have had time to move on to the sacrificials, these can be taken away and burnt or composted together.

A mixed and varied planting creates more stable systems of plants, pests and predators and prevents the spread of diseases. Seen here are Geranium pratense *(blue),* G. psilotemon *(magenta), marjoram and lady's mantle (*Alchemilla mollis*).*

163

SOME REMEDIES FOR COMMON PESTS

Ants

Black ants do not sting but may bite; red ants sting. They are all attracted to the honeydew excreted by aphids. Black ants milk, protect and move aphids to better feeding. They overwinter aphids and eggs in their nests. They may be helpful in similar ways to other pests such as scale insects, whiteflies and mealy bugs. They may prey on some other pests – citrus growers in China have used them to control caterpillars – and they may pollinate plants unbeknown to us. They uproot seedlings and even large plants with their burrowing, but the pulverized soil aids other plants, especially as it contains finely divided organic material.

The main problem is their arrival in the house or store. Strewing with one of the mints, especially spearmint or pennyroyal, will repel them. Growing the mints or tansy near their entrance point will also help. Non-drying sticky bands are a very effective deterrent on fruit trees.

Aphids

Generally considered a plague, these often do little real harm. They suck sap and spread virus diseases, but usually just take surplus nutrients without affecting overall growth. There are many different aphids – some are specific to a few plants, while others are less particular.

Chives discourage aphids on many plants, especially chrysanthemums, sunflowers and tomatoes. Nasturtiums, although themselves attacked, will keep broccoli clear of aphids. Ladybirds and hoverflies are the best controls, so grow attractant plants like *Limnanthes douglasii*, buckwheat and *Convolvulus tricolor*.

Children are one of the worst pests in the garden – this is a fact which should not be overlooked, despite any anthropomorphic sympathy. They are capable of doing incalculable damage, not only stealing fruit but breaking branches and despoiling much more. High, thorny hedges of bramble are the best solution. Himalayan giant blackberry needs space but will stop a runaway car. It produces prolifically. Bedford giant is a more lax-growing variety, best wound through other trees and shrubs. Any bramble will do, though the hybrids like loganberries tend to be bristly rather than thorny. Shrub and climbing roses, *Berberis* and *Pyracantha* are all impossible to penetrate. Worcesterberry has several advantages: it

roots where the tips touch, it suckers, produces vicious thorns and grows only to head height.

Sacrificial crops in the hedges may not fob children off so much as draw them to your garden – a better policy might be to donate some fruit trees to some verge or waste land a little way down the road.

Flea beetles

These make small holes in the leaves of brassicas, especially turnips, radishes and Chinese cabbage. They dislike moist conditions, so interplanting lettuce or spinach deters them. They can be discouraged with mint, catnip, wormwood, elderberry, tomato or bergamot; bits of these scattered around may be just as effective and will not compete with the crop. Flypaper waved close overhead thins flea beetles out.

Mosquitos

Gnats, flies and true mosquitos are all repelled by the same herbs – rue, tansy and lemon verbena. Sophora, elder and walnut trees will also discourage them.

Mice

These are pests with little good to be said for them except that they are not rats. Strong herbs such as mint or the camphor plant, alliums, elder, euphorbias, wormwood and corn chamomile repel them, as do the everlasting pea (*Lathyrus latifolius*) and such spring bulbs as *Narcissus*, *Scilla* and *Muscari*. Grain may be protected with leaves of dwarf elder which have a strange vanilla scent and purgative properties. Cats, traps and poison are all effective and needed for health and hygiene.

Moles

Anyone who can find a really effective mole deterrent will be rich and famous. Euphorbias and castor oil plants are often suggested in literature, but I have yet to see first-hand proof. Elderberry twigs are another possibility. Dogs and cats can be trained to wait and catch moles.

Nematodes

Eelworms cause a lot damage but can be repelled by marigolds (both the pot variety

An example of passive pest control! The 'Albertine' rose hides and feeds birds and larger predators; the lady's mantle (Alchemilla mollis) *at ground level performs the same service for ground beetles and others.*

Shasta daisies (Chrysanthemum maximum) *and goldenrod* (Solidago spp.) *are tough plants which are remarkably trouble free (apart from their spreading nature). Despite poor soil and inattention, almost every bit of root will produce a strong plant with masses of flowers for beneficial insects.*

and *Tagetes* spp.), sage, asparagus, petunias and dahlias. High levels of organic matter in the soil, especially compost, will help control them by increasing the number and variety of predatory fungi. Dug in oats or barley protect roots and potatoes against root knot eelworm. Flax, charlock, mustard and beans give off root exudations that kill nematodes, as does *Tagetes minuta*, the Mexican marigold. Onions grown before beets prevent them being attacked, and the proximity of asparagus kills the *Trichodorus* eelworm which preys on tomatoes. Potatoes can be protected from eelworms by another marigold, *Tagetes sinuata*.

Slugs and snails
Thorny, prickly and evergreen plants with dusty, dry soil underneath, onions, rosemary, wormwood and oak leaves discourage them. Traps of saucers of beer lure them to drown. It must be real beer and twigs must be put in so that beetles can escape up them. Any cool, dark, moist place attracts slugs and snails, so orange skins, marrow shells and wet carpet or flat bits of rotten wood will make excellent traps. Salt, lime, woodash and soot all kill these pests quickly in dry weather.

Spider mites
There are different species indoors and out. Many can be dislodged or made uncomfortable with jets of water and high humidity. Rhubarb nearby is said to keep them off aquilegias. Garlic, chilli pepper and soap sprays have some effect, derris more so. A two per cent solution of coriander oil is claimed to kill them. The commercially available predator *Phytoseilis persimilis* is very effective indoors under cover.

Whitefly
Most often a problem in the greenhouse, whitefly can be discouraged with *Tagetes*, nasturtiums and burning oak leaves. They are more prevalent on tomatoes when they suffer phosphorus or magnesium deficiency. Brassicas are often bothered by them in the open and marigolds and nasturtiums are good deterrents. *Nicandra physaloides*, Peruvian cherry, may repel whiteflies indoors or out. The predator *Encarsia formosa* is very effective. Numbers can also be thinned by running a vacuum cleaner over the plant.

Wireworms
These can be killed with a green manure crop of flax; suppressed by white mustard, buckwheat and woad; or trapped with bits of potatoes or roots baiting empty, half-buried tins.

PLANTS THAT WERE ONCE USED TO MAKE INSECTICIDAL SPRAYS

Home-made pesticides are now illegal in the UK, but all the following plants were once used in general-purpose sprays. I include this information for historical interest, and because the plants themselves may also have useful companion effects in repelling pests.

Allium sativum
Garlic emulsion will kill aphids and onion flies. It has also been used against codling moths, snails, root maggots, Japanese beetles, carrot root fly and peach leaf curl.

Narcissus spp.
Daffodils repel rodents and have been used against cabbage worms, Colorado beetles and squash bugs.

Nicotiana spp.
Many of these are sticky, especially *N. sylvestris*, woodland tobacco, and so can trap small insects and flies. They were much used in the past to make nicotine, a powerful insecticide that kills almost anything.

Pelargonium spp.
In the US these have been used as sprays against cabbage moths, corn earworms and Japanese beetles.

Sabadilla dust
Sabadilla, a lily relative, has been used against grasshoppers, cornworms, cornborers, army worms, silkworms, melon worms, blister beetles, greenhouse leaf tier, chinch bugs, lygus bugs, harlequin bugs, codling moths, webworms, aphids, cabbage loopers and squash bugs since the sixteenth century. It is now unknown, unobtainable and illegal in the UK, but available in the US.

Spergula arvensis
Sprays made from spurry have been used against aphids, cutworms, caterpillars and rootworms.

Tansy
The spray has been used against aphids, cabbage worms, squash bugs, Colorado beetles, Japanese beetles and striped cucumber beetles.

Ripening Merryweather damsons protected from pests and diseases by tansy.

Disease control

Organic, biodynamic and companion methods of disease control depend primarily on the production of healthy plants. If they are growing strongly with no stress from water shortage or nutrient deficiency, then the presence of some disease will rarely affect the final result a great deal. Good garden hygiene to remove infected material combined with frequent and regular observation should mean you spot trouble before it spreads. Care should be taken not to be a plant hypochondriac: many perfectly healthy plants look very unhappy at the end of the season. Potatoes, for instance, look horrible as the leaves senesce and die back and cause many novices to believe (erroneously) that they have an attack of blight. Roses look awful if rain soaks the flowers, and plums drop their leaves apparently early.

Sensible use of companion planting and organic methods means few plants will suffer total failure, but some direct action may occasionally be warranted. Sulphur dust, Bordeaux mixture, waterglass (sodium silicate), sodium bicarbonate, seaweed extracts and herbal sprays can be of benefit in reducing attacks of disease and are all permitted under organic standards as they do little harm to soil life, though they may be illegal used in this way in the UK.

Mildews are fungi of broadly two types, powdery and downy. Generally speaking, the powdery forms do less damage than the downy, grey-matted ones. They attack plants under stress, 'eating' from the outside. The commonest causes are plants being too dry at the roots, and stagnant air. Good growing conditions suitable to the plant, careful pruning and training to allow access of air and light will do much to alleviate mildews. Growing any of the alliums nearby will offer some protection, but this needs time to work. Removing diseased material helps. Wood ashes, equisetum tea, seaweed and nettle sprays make plants tougher and more resistant to disease.

Bonfires

These are a necessary evil – some material is too thorny or diseased to compost or use to build wildlife shelters. It should preferably be burnt piecemeal in a stove to warm the house. If you are about to have a bonfire, please drag it to bits and burn it a little at a time. This will save any hedgehogs and other creatures from a horrible death and a small, hot bonfire is far better ecologically than a great smouldering pile.

A bonfire burns best when the air can get underneath it, so use some bricks and old metal posts to raise it off the ground. Try to wait till the wind is light, steady and blowing away from anything that may be harmed. Light a small, fierce fire and add material steadily as it burns away. When there are only glowing lumps, quench the flames with just enough water to put them out, but no more. Save the lumps of charcoal for barbecues and the ashes for the gooseberries, roses and cooking apples.

COMPOSTING

This is at the heart of good gardening. The compost heap is the furnace which converts waste into fertility and soil health. Everything that has lived can be composted, but be wary of fats, meats and bones, as these attract vermin. Woody, thorny material is not easily composted and should be omitted, as should conifer and evergreen leaves. Include as many herbs as possible, with the exception of wormwood, which slows down the process. Comfrey, nettles and animal manures are especially beneficial to the composting and human urine makes one of the very best stimulators. Weeds are best wilted in the sun beforehand and, if they are seeding, put in the middle of the heap.

Herbs recommended by Rudolph Steiner to encourage the micro-organisms in a compost heap to thrive are chamomile, dandelions, stinging nettles, valerian and yarrow. He also suggests oak bark. These can be obtained ready prepared from biodynamic suppliers. The Maye E. Bruce compost stimulator, sold as Q. R. Compost Activator, uses a similar recipe with honey. These work, but in my experience they are no more effective than a few shovels of poultry manure! The most important ingredients are sufficient but not too much air and moisture, with enough bulk to heat the whole thing up.

To make compost effectively a big quantity is required. The optimum size of bin is that formed by four pallets (like those lifted on fork lift trucks) tied at the corners to make a neat bin, a bit less than a cubic metre (yard) in capacity. Smaller bins do not do as well, larger no better. The wood will last a few years longer if soaked in a preservative, but this may affect the microlife adversely. Once a bin is made the material needs to be accumulated – the more the better as it disappears, or at least four fifths will. When you have gathered an enormous amount, mix it all up, make it moist and fill the bin more than full, stack it high. Cover with a lid or carpet and leave for a week.

After a week, unpack, remix and remake it with the inside outside and vice versa. If it looks dry with white mould, wet it more. If it is wet and slimy, mix in dry grass, leaves or straw. Leave it for another week, then repeat this process.

Now leave the compost for about five or six months, then sieve and use it; save the sievings to inoculate the next heap. If you are making your first heap, scrounge some sievings from an established heap to help yours start – but be absolutely certain there is no danger of importing clubroot: you will never get rid of it.

It is very bad planning to site compost bins under pine trees and to a lesser extent under other conifers, as they exude substances that arrest decomposition. Conversely, birch and elder have a beneficial effect and make good screens around the bins.

Well-made garden compost is so valuable that it is wasteful to dig it in wholesale – it should be saved for putting in planting holes and for dressing hungry plants. Mixed with leaf mould or peat it makes an excellent potting mixture, though even well-made compost always seems to have some weed seeds to annoy.

This clematis ('Blue Azure') is unlikely to suffer from diseases now that it is established, with its head in the sun but the roots well down in the cool shade provided by the buddleia.

Make every effort to recycle and obtain as much and as many varied materials for composting as possible. Nothing makes for more healthy plants in a healthy soil as the frequent addition of copious amounts of well-made compost. The best companions for your plants are the remains of all those that have gone before.

On reflection, it becomes apparent to me that a garden is not a thing so much as a process. The history and potential of each plant is interconnected with that of all the others that exist or have ever existed around and about it. As one plant prospers, another fails and more are waiting in the wings for their turn.

USDA PLANT HARDINESS ZONE MAP

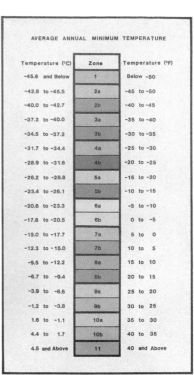

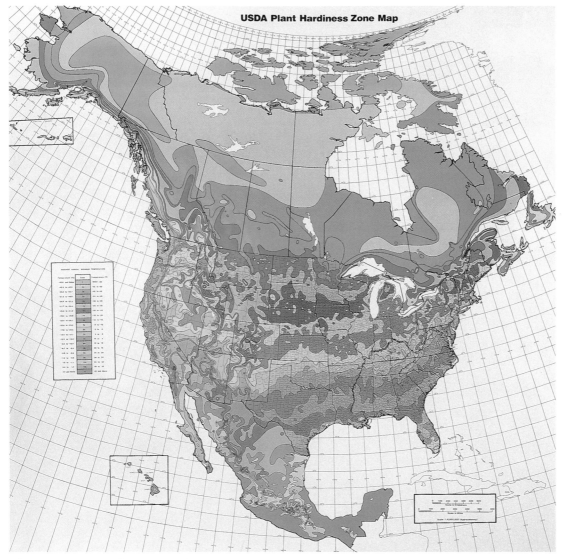

Photo: courtesy Agricultural Research Service, USDA

PHOTOGRAPHER'S NOTE

Many of the photographs in this book were taken in the author's garden. I would also like to thank all the other people who have allowed me to photograph their gardens for this book: Janet Allen, Mr and Mrs Burnett, Beth Chatto, Kate Campbell, Mr and Mrs Coode-Adams, Natalie Finch, Will Giles, Mrs Anne Hoellering, Deborah Kellaway, Maggie and James Lythgoe, Mr and Mrs Ravenshear, and John and Caroline Stevens. I would also like to thank David Robertson for his invaluable support.

USEFUL ADDRESSES – UK

Those organizations that have facilities for visitors are marked thus *

The Bio-Dynamic Agricultural Association, Woodman Lane, Clent, Stourbridge, West Midlands DY9 9PX

* The Centre for Alternative Technology, The Quarry, Machynlleth, Powys, SY20 9AZ

The Good Gardeners' Association, Arkley Manor, Arkley, Herts EN5 3HJ

* The Henry Doubleday Research Association, National Centre for Organic Gardening, Ryton on Dunsmore, Coventry CV8 3LG

The McHarrison Society, 25 Tamar Way, Wokingham, Berks RG11 9UB

* The Northern Horticultural Society, Harlow Car Gardens, Crag Lane, Otley Road, Harrogate, W. Yorks HG3 1QB

The Royal Horticultural Society, Vincent Square, London SW1P 2LX
* Wisley, Woking, Surrey GU23 6QB

The Soil Association, 86-88 Colston Street, Bristol, Avon BS1 5BB
  British Organic Farmers, 86 Colston Street, Bristol, Avon BS1 5BB
  Organic Growers Association, 86 Colston Street, Bristol, Avon BS1 5BB
  Elm Farm Research Centre, Hamstead Marshall, Newbury, Berks RG15 0HR

WWOOF (Working Weekends On Organic Farms), 19 Bradford Road, Lewes, Sussex BN7 1RB

USEFUL ADDRESSES – US

Organizations marked with '*' have information or exhibits for visitors, but since many have small staffs, appointments are recommended or required.

* Bio-Dynamic Farming and Gardening Association, P.O. Box 550, Kimberton, Pennsylvania 19442
Tel: (215) 935-7797 Fax: (215) 983-3196

IAA (Institute for Alternative Agriculture), 9200 Edmonston Road, Greenbelt, Maryland 20770-1551
Tel: (301) 441-8777 Fax: (301) 220-0164

MOFGA (Maine Organic Farmers and Gardeners Association), P.O. Box 2176, Augusta, Maine 04338
Tel: (207) 622-3118

* Michael Fields Agricultural Institute, W2493 County Road ES, East Troy, Wisconsin 53120
Tel: (414) 642-3303 Fax: (414) 642-4028

* Nature Farming Research and Development Foundation, 6495 Santa Rosa Road, Lompoc, California 93436
Tel: (805) 737-1536 Fax: (805) 736-9599

Naropa Institute, 2130 Arapaho, Boulder, Colorado 80301
Tel: (303) 444-0202 Fax: (303) 444-0410

Natural Organic Farmers Association of New York, P.O. Box 21, South Butler, NY 13154
Tel: (315) 365-2299

NPSAS (Northern Plains Sustainable Agricultural Society), P.O. Box 36, Maida, North Dakota 58255
Tel: (701) 256-2424

* The Peaceable Kingdom School, P.O. Box 313, Washington on the Brazos, Texas 77880
Tel: (409) 878-2353

* Rodale Institute Research Center, 611 Siegfriedale Road, Kutztown, Pennsylvania 19530
Tel: (215) 683-6383 Fax: (215) 683-8548

* Stony Brook-Millstone Watershed Association, Attn: Sustainable Agriculture, R.D. 2, Box 263A, Titus Mill Road, Pennington, New Jersey 08534
Tel: (609) 737-3735

BIBLIOGRAPHY

These are books worth looking out for. Although they are not all directly concerned with companion planting, they contain much useful and relevant advice. Several of them have long been out of print and will have to be unearthed from libraries.

Agricultural Development and Advisory Service, *Plant Physiological Disorders* (HMSO, 1985)

Allan, Mea *The Gardener's Book of Weeds* (Macdonald & Jane's, 1978)

Bruce, Maye E. *From Vegetable Waste to Fertile Soil* (Pearson, 1940)

Buczacki, Stefan *Ground Rules for Gardeners* (Collins, 1986)

Carson, Rachel *Silent Spring* (Hamish Hamilton, 1962)

Chancellor, R.J. *The Identification of Weed Seedlings of Farm and Garden* (Blackwell Scientific Publications, n.d.)

Cobbett, William *Treatise on Gardening* (1821)

Cooper, Shewell *The Complete Vegetable Grower* (Faber & Faber, 1967)

Drabble, Hilda *Plant Ecology* (Edward Arnold, 1937)

Elliott, R.H. *Clifton Park System of Farming* (Faber & Faber, 1943)

Franck, Gertrud *Companion Planting: Successful Gardening the Organic Way* (Thorsons, 1983)

Genders, Roy *Perfume in the Garden* (Museum Press, n.d.)

Gregg, R.B. & Philbrick, H. *Companion Plants* (Watkins, 1967). This was based on two earlier works, Gregg's *Primer of Companion Planting* ('Bio Dynamics' Vol. III, No. 1, 1943) and Philbrick's *Herbs, Their Part in Good Gardening* ('The Forerunner', Vol. V, No. 1, n.d.)

Hardy Plant Society, *The Plant Finder*

Harrison, Masefield & Wallace, *The Oxford Book of Food Plants* (Peerage Book, 1969)

Hatfield, A.W. *How to Enjoy your Weeds* (Muller, 1969)

Hillier's Manual of Trees and Shrubs (5th edition, David & Charles, 1981)

Hills, L.D. *Good Fruit Guide* (HDRA, 1984)

—— *Organic Gardening* (Penguin, 1977)

HMSO *The Diagnosis of Mineral Deficiencies in Plants* (1943)

Hunter, B.T. *Gardening without Poisons* (Hamish Hamilton, 1965)

Huxley, Anthony *Plant and Planet* (Allen Lane, 1974)

Jeavons, J. *How to Grow More Vegetables* (Tenspeed Press, 1979)

Larkcom, Joy *Vegetables from Small Gardens* (Faber & Faber, 1986)

Ordish, G. *The Constant Pest* (Peter Davies, n.d.)

Ormerod, E.A. *Manual of Injurious Insects and Methods of Prevention* (Simpson, Marshall, Hamilton & Kent, 1890)

Pfeiffer, Ehrenfried *Formative Forces in Crystallization* (Rudolf Steiner, 1936)

—— *Practical Guide to the Use of Bio-Dynamic Preparations* (Ruldolf Steiner, 1935)

—— *Soil Fertility, Renewal and Preservation* (Faber & Faber, 1947)

—— *Weeds and what they can tell you* (Rodale, 1981)

Philbrick, H. see under Gregg, R.B., above

Riotte, L. *Secrets of Companion Planting* (Garden Way, 1975)

Robbins, Crafts & Raynor *Weed Control* (McGraw Hill, 1942)

Russell, John *Soil Conditions and Plant Growth* (8th edition, Longman, 1954)

Schuphan, Werner *Nutritional Values in Crops and Plants* (Faber & Faber, 1965)

Soper, John *Bio-Dynamic Gardening* (Bio-Dynamic Agricultural Association, 1983)

US Department of Agriculture *Soil* (1957)

Willis, Stephen J. *Weed Control in Farm and Garden* (Vinton, n.d.)

Verey, Rosemary *The Scented Garden* (Van Nostrand Reinhold, 1981)

Yepsen, R.B. (ed.) *Organic Plant Protection* (Rodale, 1976)

INDEX